GROWING
UP

DATE DUE

GROWING UP

How to Be a Disciple

Who Makes Disciples

ROBBY GALLATY

PUBLISHING
NASHVILLE, TENNESSEE

Published by B&H Publishing Group
Nashville, Tennessee

Dewey Decimal Classification: 248.84
Subject Heading: DISCIPLESHIP / DISCIPLESHIP
TRAINING / CHRISTIAN LIFE

Cover design by B&H Publishing Group.
Icons by Aleksei_Derin/vectorstock.
Author photo by Jo McVey Photography LLC.

1 2 3 4 5 6 · 25 24 23 22

Book 1
Growing Up
Psalm 1:1–2

How happy is the one who does not walk in
the advice of the wicked or stand in the pathway
with sinners or sit in the company of mockers!
Instead, his delight is in the Lord's instruction,
and he meditates on it day and night.

Book 2
Firmly Planted
Psalm 1:3a

He is like a tree planted beside flowing streams . . .

Book 3
Bearing Fruit
Psalm 1:3b

. . . that bears its fruit in its season and whose
leaf does not wither. Whatever he does prospers.

To Chris Swain

No one I know lived out the principles
in this series more than you. You lived every
day with the end in mind. Your investment
in pastors, believers, friends, and family
will reverberate for years to come.

CONTENTS

C.L.O.S.E.R.

FOREWORD

So what do you do when a 6'6" 290-pound thieving drug-dealing pill addict trained in Brazilian Jiu-Jitsu is standing next to you on a Sunday morning in a church gathering? My thought is that you become that guy's friend as soon as possible! So one Sunday, years ago, I had the God-ordained, God-orchestrated privilege of meeting Robby Gallaty.

Simply put, the Lord's hand on this brother was evident from the moment I met him. Robby had just become a follower of Christ, and his zeal for Christ was not just clear; it was contagious. Before long, I had the privilege of baptizing him, which is quite a story in and of itself (just imagine this 6'6" 290-pound man slipping on his way down into the baptistery and falling straight toward you, causing water to splash over onto the choir like a wave pool out of control). Every week, Robby and I would meet for Chinese food over lunch. We would walk together through God's Word and pray together for one another. I can still remember sitting over General Tso's chicken watching Robby write down every single truth I shared with him on the napkins at Mr. Wang's. Then he would take that truth and not only apply it in his life, but also teach it in others' lives. I visibly watched this brother soak in the gospel as he spread the gospel on a weekly basis. From the start, Robby Gallaty was growing as a disciple of

Jesus while simultaneously giving his life to making disciples of Jesus.

After all, this is the essence of what Christianity is all about, right? In Jesus's initial call to four men standing by the Sea of Galilee, we see that the inevitable overflow of being a disciple of Jesus is making disciples of Jesus. "Follow me," Jesus said, "and I will make you fishers of men" (Matt. 4:19). This was a promise: Jesus would take his disciples and turn them into disciple-makers. And this was a command: he would call each of his disciples at the end of Matthew to go and make disciples of all nations, baptizing them and teaching them to obey him (Matt. 28:19–20). From the start, God's simple design has been for every single disciple of Jesus to make disciples who make disciples who make disciples until the gospel spreads to all peoples on the planet.

Yet we have subtly and tragically taken this costly command of Christ to go, baptize, and teach all nations and mutated it into a comfortable call for Christians to come, be baptized, and listen in one location. If you were to ask individual Christians today what it means either to be a disciple or to make disciples, you would likely get jumbled thoughts, ambiguous answers, and probably even some blank stares. In all our activity as Christians and with all our resources in the church, we are practically ignoring the commission of Christ. Evangelism is relegated to a dreaded topic, discipleship is reduced to a canned program, and the majority of the church is currently sitting sidelined in a spectator mentality that delegates disciple-making to pastors and professionals, ministers and missionaries.

But this is not the way it's supposed to be. Jesus has invited all of us to be a part of his plan. He has designed each of his people to know all of his joy as we share all of his love, spread all of his Word, and multiply all of his life among all of the peoples of the earth. So how do we do this? How do we as disciples practically, daily, passionately, and plainly make disciples?

The significance of that question leads to my sheer enthusiasm over the book you hold in your hands. Here you will find a biblical, practical, reproducible, and simple starting point for growing as a disciple of Jesus and giving your life to making disciples of Jesus. This is not mere theory you are holding onto right now. This is tried and true practice. I know it is because I've seen it in action. I've walked personally with Robby Gallaty through the practices that are found in this book. Words cannot express how grateful I am for the time that he and I shared reading and studying the Word with one another, praying and weeping for the world on our knees next to each other, and sharing life alongside one another as we spread the gospel together in New Orleans. Since that time, Robby has gone on to pastor two disciple-making churches, including Brainerd Baptist Church, where he now shepherds a people who don't just talk about disciple-making; they do it.

And so I want to encourage you as clearly as I possibly can. Please don't read this book. Instead, do it. If you only read what you find here, you will remain mired in a stagnant, stale, self-consumed Christianity that misses the whole purpose for which you have been saved. Christian, you have been created and called by God to grow as a disciple and to give your life to making disciples. And this cause, more than any other, is worth giving your life to. It's worth it for billions of people who do not yet know the joy of following Jesus. And it's worth it for you and me, because we were made to be disciples who make disciples who make disciples until the day when we see the face of the One we follow, and together with all nations we exalt his supremacy and experience his satisfaction for all of eternity. My prayer is that this resource from my friend and brother might be used in the hand of God to hasten the coming of that day.

Dr. David Platt
pastor, McLean Bible Church
author of *Radical* and *Follow Me*

INTRODUCTION

The gospel came to you because it was heading to someone else. God never intended for your salvation to be an end, but a beginning. God saved you to be a conduit through whom His glorious, life-changing gospel would flow to others. You are a link in the chain of 2 Timothy 2:2, which says, "What you have heard from me in the presence of many witnesses entrust to faithful men who will be able to teach others also."

Let me begin this book by saying thank you. By picking up this resource, you are communicating a number of things. You want to grow in your relationship with God. You take Jesus's command in Matthew 28:19 to make disciples seriously. You have a burden to leave an eternal legacy by investing in the lives of others. Perhaps you yearn for someone to invest in you. Regardless of the reasons, you are beginning a journey toward a deeper relationship with Christ.

Growing Up is a resource that has the potential to change your life. How can I say this?

1. This book is built on solid biblical principles. God's Word, which He promised would never return void, imparts faith and produces a life change.

2. These principles have been tried and tested over the past decade in various discipleship groups (D-Groups).
3. My life has been impacted immensely through discipling relationships. I share my story of how God radically saved me from a life of drugs and alcohol in chapter 1.

One Warning

This book should not be read and then abandoned on a shelf. As a manual for making disciples, it is a resource you will use for years to come. Underline in it, write in the margins, interact with it, and meditate on it. You are not learning this information for only yourself, although you will definitely benefit from it. You are learning it for all the people you will disciple in the future, those who will receive the gospel because it flowed to them through you.

As you read, please take notes. Did you know that you forget 40 percent of what you hear within twenty minutes, and you retain only about 20 percent within one week?[1] If you don't write something down, you will forget it. How else will you pass on what you have learned, unless you record it? Where would we be if the apostles hadn't written down the Word of God for us to read today?

One Qualification

Every time I speak on discipleship, I am asked afterward, "Where do I begin?" or, "How do I get started?" After answering these questions hundreds of times, I decided to create a road map for others to follow. As you read through this book, you will find that I purposely spent only a little time expounding philosophy, theory, and the necessity for making disciples. That's because men and women far more experienced than I have already written extensively on this subject. (These resources are mentioned throughout the book.)

Numerous books define discipleship, outline objectives for making disciples, and provide biblical evidence from both the Old and New Testaments. Many are invaluable resources. However, after reading these books, I was often left wondering, "Now what?" I have a sneaking suspicion that I am not the only one asking that question. I've come to realize that when people don't know what to do, they don't do anything.

Prayerfully, this resource will aid in putting feet to your faith through mapping out a plan for investing in others. It is purposefully practical, easy to use, and simple to follow.

The DNA of Discipleship

From time to time, people ask me, "What was the difference that made the difference at Brainerd Baptist Church?" The answer is easy: discipleship.

When I arrived as senior pastor at Brainerd in 2008, only a handful of people were meeting in intentional D-Groups, or a group of three to five people who meet weekly for the express purpose of becoming disciples who make disciples.

Beginning with my pastoral staff, I redesigned the weekly three-hour business/staff meeting into a D-Group, focusing on Scripture reading and memorization (we memorized the entire book of 2 Timothy in 2009) and extended prayer times. The atmosphere changed overnight.

After a year of meeting, I challenged the staff to identify two or three people to meet with in a D-Group (men with men, and women with women). During my second year at Brainerd, we estimated that one hundred people were meeting in D-Groups. In 2014, we expect to have more than one thousand people meeting in D-Groups throughout our fellowship. Keep in mind, the individuals meeting are in addition to small-group Bible study and Sunday school attendance. Sunday school classes and small groups are the seedbeds for building D-Group relationships.

Our church's mission statement, "Deliver, Disciple, and Deploy," was formative in shaping the DNA of our congregation. People in a church will always celebrate what the pastor celebrates. If the pastor celebrates bodies, bucks, or buildings, the people will perceive those as most important, and they will become the measure of success. However, when the pastor highlights restoring relationships, transforming lives, and maturing believers within the D-Groups, people will soon desire to participate in a group. When I started celebrating what God was doing in D-Groups, our people quickly followed.

How to Use the Material

If you are serious about being a disciple of Jesus Christ—really, truly serious—you will become a part of a D-Group. Again, Jesus Himself established this model for us. He formed and personally led the first D-Group—and it worked. The men who emerged from that group took the gospel to the world, and ultimately, they laid down their lives for Christ.

A D-Group creates an atmosphere for fellowship, encouragement, and accountability, and it is an environment where God can work. A healthy D-Group has three purposes: to help you grow in your relationship with Christ, give a defense for your faith, and guide others in their relationship with Christ.

You may be thinking, "How do I get in a D-Group? Where can I find one?" Ask your pastor or another church leader about the availability of groups in your church. If your church doesn't have such groups, find a mature Christian who is willing to lead the group and two or three other believers who want to grow in their walk with the Lord, and start a group. Who knows? God may want to use *you* to begin this movement in your church. If you want to know where to start, feel free to check out some resources we have created at replicate.org/dgroup.

As you mature in your faith, those in the group can eventually start and lead other groups. This book will equip you to do just that.

Book Outline

To get the most out of this resource, review each chapter in your D-Group. Watch for three pairs of synonymous terms that will be used interchangeably:

- disciple-making and discipleship
- mentor and discipler
- mentee and disciple

Growing Up is divided into two sections. The first three chapters build a case for the necessity of making disciples. Chapter 4 deals with training yourself to become godly. The remaining six chapters, if incorporated into your life, will aid in developing a CLOSER walk with Christ. This walk will help you . . .

- communicate with God through prayer
- learn to understand and apply God's Word to your life
- obey God's commands
- store God's Word in your heart
- evangelize (share Christ with others)
- renew yourself spiritually every day

Regularly practicing even one of these disciplines will increase your spiritual fervor. The more of them you cultivate in your life, the closer you will grow to the Lord, and the more you will become like Christ. If you practice all of them, you will see exponential growth in your life. Whether you are a new believer or have been in church your entire life, these practices will produce tangible results in godliness and fruitfulness—*if* you are disciplined enough to stick with them. The key to sticking with them is being accountable to someone else. Accountability is provided through a D-Group.

Moving Forward

An ideal D-Group (a concept discussed in chapter 3) consists of three to five people meeting together weekly. The meeting place is insignificant: it can be someone's home, a restaurant, a break room at work, or at church. To fulfill its purpose and be profitable, each meeting must be focused on the disciple-building activities discussed throughout this book.

Before beginning any disciple-making relationship, expectations between the mentee and the mentor must be clearly discussed and understood. Both parties must sign a disciple-making covenant, agreeing to take the relationship seriously. (A copy of this covenant can be found in Appendix 1.) Stress the importance of attending weekly meetings and completing all assigned work as you distribute the document. You can use the Personal Faith Inventory found in Appendix 2 as a platform for discussion in the group's first meeting.

The entire discipleship process is outlined in the Afterword and Appendix 9. At some point during the process, each participant should lead a session. Without incorporating this step, many may not feel equipped to replicate the process, and as a result, never lead their own group.

This discipleship system is reproducible and designed to be duplicated. Jesus commanded us to go into the world and "make disciples" (Matt. 28:19). He followed this command by providing instructions for developing disciples, "teaching them [future disciples] to observe all that I have commanded you" (Matt. 28:20).

As you study and grow, remember that you are not merely learning for your own benefit, but also for the benefit of others. Again, you must take notes. How else will you pass on the information you have learned?

Guiding others in their walk with Christ is a joy many overlook. The first and foremost way to make disciples is to become a disciple, and the only way to teach others effectively is to continue as a lifelong learner. We are closest to Christ when we are doing what He has commanded us to do, and the best way to learn is to teach.

Okay, I'm In. What's Next?

I have learned that the secrets to the Christian life are the obvious. While I would love to uncover some hidden truth undiscovered by men and women of old, God has already communicated a blueprint for spiritual growth in His Word. The purpose of this book is to explain that blueprint and motivate you to follow it.

After spending the last decade of my life being discipled and discipling others, the six practices discussed in this book (C.L.O.S.E.R.) have proven to be irreplaceable in spiritual development. When practiced diligently, these crucial disciplines provide a springboard for even deeper disciplines to flourish, such as silence, solitude, frugality, fasting, and worship. When these disciplines are pursued, the desire for going even deeper with God will be birthed in your soul.

Don't Attempt It Alone

The very first disciples—the twelve hand-picked by Jesus Himself—were a part of a group. This is the model that Jesus, the architect of discipleship, established for us to follow. Our all-wise Savior (who, by the way, knows more about this than we do) recognized something: *being His disciple is not easy.* Therefore, we should not attempt it alone. We need fellowship with other Christ-followers. We need encouragement from them. And, perhaps most importantly, we need to be accountable to them.

Additionally, we who choose to pursue discipleship need something else: an example to follow—a living, walking, talking disciple of Jesus Christ. We must have someone to guide us along the way, someone to set some footprints in the sand of the Christian life for us to follow, someone to hold us to following them.

Paul understood this truth and willingly assumed the responsibility of leading others. To the Philippian church he wrote: *"Brothers, join in imitating me, and keep your eyes on those who walk according to the example you have in us"* (Phil. 3:17).

The word *imitate* simply means to copy. Paul didn't mean that the Philippian Christians should become clones of him. Rather, he is asking the Philippians to follow him in his pursuit of Jesus. He wanted them to emulate his general conduct and way of life, a life that walked in Jesus's footprints. Hence, his ultimate goal was not for them to follow him, but Christ, as Paul explained in his first letter to the church at Corinth, writing, *"Follow my example, as I follow the example of Christ"* (1 Cor. 11:1 NIV).

Your success in the Christian life is significantly linked to how well you walk with other Christians. When he said, *"Walk according to the example . . ."* (Phil. 3:17), Paul used wording that described a row

8

of soldiers, marching in perfect order. Similarly, C. S. Lewis likened the church of Jesus Christ to a fleet of ships sailing in formation.[2] The essence of discipleship is one believer leading others to follow their course, as they follow Christ. Confucius captured this idea: "Tell me and I will forget; show me and I may remember; involve me and I will understand."[3]

Weekly Outline

The objective of each D-Group meeting is to understand new truths, reinforce principles and precepts, and apply what is taught. Read and discuss a chapter each week with your group. Lesson plans for each chapter can be found on our website: http://replicate. org. The questions throughout the chapter will serve as discussion points for your sessions. Encourage group members to highlight insights gleaned from the chapter, offer thoughtful comments, and ask questions. There are never any foolish questions. All group members should feel comfortable asking anything. Remember that the goal is not only to learn new information, but also to be transformed by what you are learning. Expect to be challenged every week by what you have read.

Online Resources

You can find numerous videos, resources, outlines, and tools to assist in your discipling journey on our website: http://replicate.org. These videos answer commonly asked questions about discipleship and coach you through the process of investing in others. Additionally, you will find interviews from various disciple-makers. Make sure you sign up for our newsletter as well, to keep up with upcoming events and training sessions.

Begin with the End in Mind

The purpose of the D-Group is for the participants to be conformed to the image of Christ. Paul, in his letter to the Roman church, said, *"Do not be conformed to this world, but be transformed by the renewal of your mind . . ."* (Rom. 12:2). How are we transformed? Through the mind. The word *transformed* is in the present tense, signifying a gradual, ongoing change. What is surprising is that the word is in the passive voice. God is the author and finisher of the change.

How does the transformation take place? His Spirit uses circumstances, situations, and His Word to produce an inner change of mind, which leads to a life transformation. David testified, *"I have hidden your word in my heart that I might not sin against you"* (Ps. 119:11 NIV). In a similar fashion, Paul said, *"Set your minds on things that are above, not on things that are on earth"* (Col. 3:2). You've heard the expression, "You are what you eat." Biblically, we could say, "You are what you think." Hence, every chapter is centered on the Word of God.

Let's get started.

Chapter 1

THE DIFFERENCE THAT MADE THE DIFFERENCE

"And what you have heard from me in the presence of many witnesses entrust to faithful men who will be able to teach others also."
2 Timothy 2:2

"Ultimately, each church will be evaluated by only one thing—its disciples."
Neil Cole

I thought I had hit rock bottom when I stole $15,000 from my parents. I was a twenty-five-year-old drug dealer, hopelessly addicted to prescription medications. The police were on my trail, and my prosperous life suddenly fell apart.

Fast-forward eleven years. Today, I have a godly wife and two sons, and I am privileged to serve as pastor of a thriving congregation. I have seen God move in my life, in my family's life, and in the lives of thousands of people all around the world. I have been blessed beyond measure.

Here is the million-dollar question: how can a thieving, drug-dealing pill addict undergo such a radical transformation in so little time—a mere eleven years? What could produce this drastic change?

The answer to this question is, first and foremost, the power and grace of God. This change has come about because of God's marvelous, miraculous working in my life. But there is something else, a human factor:

I have been powerfully impacted by godly men who were willing to sacrifice their time to hold me accountable and personally disciple me in the Christian life.

These men invested in me as Paul invested in Timothy, to whom he referred as his son in the faith. Paul's model in 2 Timothy mirrors the work of these unselfish mentors who guided me through my struggles as a new believer. Here is how it all happened.

For the first twenty-five years of my life, the Lord seemed far from me. I was born into a strict Roman Catholic family, and my parents sent me to Holy Cross High School, a Catholic school for boys in New Orleans. For me, religion consisted solely of attending Mass. Each Sunday, I sat in church and dutifully participated in the rituals, governed by a personal philosophy to do only what was best for me. Completely unconcerned with what God desired for me, I left the services with an unchanged heart—every Sunday.

I graduated from high school with a fantastic opportunity: the University of North Carolina at Greensboro awarded me a basketball scholarship. But I was in love—or so I thought—and turned the scholarship down when my girlfriend begged me to attend a college closer to home.

As I browsed the phone book to see what colleges were in the area, William Carey College jumped out at me. But when I inquired about trying out for the basketball team, I received bad news: the players had already been selected, and the roster was full.

I responded the only way a desperate eighteen-year-old boy could: I begged the coach to allow me to try out for the team. Seeing that I wasn't going away otherwise, the coach caved, and I showed him my skills. To his own surprise, Coach Steve Knight offered me a scholarship the following week.

Just two weeks after school started, my devoted girlfriend, the one for whom I had given up playing for UNC Greensboro, suddenly broke up with me. Overwhelmed with both heartache and anger, I could not see the hand of God at work in the circumstances of my life. Although I did not realize it, He was setting the stage for something glorious, a life I could never have imagined at the time.

Thanks, But No Thanks

During my second semester at William Carey, the next step in God's wonderful plan for me unfolded. In His abundant goodness and love, God brought Jeremy Brown into my life, a friend who cared enough about me to discuss what it really means to have a relationship with God. Although I refused to listen at that time, Jeremy's persistent message remained in my heart: if I would only cry out to God, Jeremy said, He would forgive me of everything in my past. By surrendering my life to God, I would find a real, meaningful relationship with Him. Seven years later, Jeremy's words would come back to me at the time I needed them most.

I graduated from college and started a computer business with two friends. For six grueling months we put everything we had into the company, but it never took off. Exhausted, dejected, and broke, we dismantled the company and each went our separate ways.

When the business folded, I felt like a failure, and turned to a realm where I was confident of success. Standing at 6'6" and 290 pounds, I was fascinated with the world of mixed martial arts. I watched extreme fighting competitions and began to train in Brazilian Jiu-Jitsu. Then, I was hired as a bouncer at a club in New Orleans, where they paid me to fight. It was exhilarating, and I felt that I was indestructible.

Life Altering Accident

I found out how wrong I was on November 22, 1999, when an eighteen-wheeler traveling sixty-five miles per hour swerved across two lanes of traffic and slammed my car into a guardrail. Doctors determined that I had two herniated discs in my neck, one herniated disc in my back, and one bulging disc in my lower back. All I knew was that I was in horrific pain. Their solution: a combination of OxyContin, Valium, Soma, and Percocet.

Having never taken drugs before, I began by precisely following the dosage instructions. But in three months, I found myself addicted to prescription painkillers. When my thirty-day supply ran low as a result of abusing the drugs, I desperately turned to dubious means of feeding my insatiable craving for more.

Two shady acquaintances introduced me to the lucrative world of dealing drugs. With my business training and experience, I quickly became successful at importing and selling illegal drugs. Trafficking heroin, cocaine, GHB, marijuana, and other dangerous substances into New Orleans enabled me to enjoy a lifestyle that most only dream about.

Downward Spiral

But in January of 2000, my world began to unravel. Rick, a former business partner and close friend,

14

overdosed on heroin and died with the needle still in his arm. Between 2000 and 2003, I lost eight friends to alcohol or drugs, while six others ended up in prison. Additionally, the police were starting to suspect me of drug-dealing and began monitoring our group.

Everything changed overnight. Suddenly, we couldn't pay the bills. The gas, water, and electricity to our house were shut off. The bill collectors continued to call until the phone was disconnected as well. To make matters even worse, I had a $180-a-day drug addiction that growled to be fed.

During that period, I stole $15,000 from my father by using his credit card to buy items online that I later pawned or sold for drug money. When my parents learned what I had done, they were totally crushed. They were well-justified in ordering me to never return to their house. Unfazed by the confrontation, I wasted the rest of my bank account on street drugs. This three-month drug binge ended with me on my parents' living room floor, penniless and begging for their help.

My next stop was a rehab program in Tijuana, Mexico, of all places. I spent ten days in an intensive recovery program involving the injection of amino acids to realign the serotonin and dopamine levels in my body. After completing the program, I moved to Mobile, Alabama, to live with my sister, and things began to improve. I even got a job as a sales manager at a gym, where I began training five days a week. One day, while foolishly attempting to squat press more than 500 pounds, I felt a familiar pain shoot through my back.

After traveling back to New Orleans for treatment, I learned that I had damaged the same disc in my back, and that I needed immediate surgery. Following the surgery, I went home with the same four pain medications that were prescribed for me after my car accident. For the next six months, I allowed these medications—substances that had caused so much hurt and heartache for my family—back into my life. Things quickly crashed for the second time. Knowing I had now reached rock bottom, I abruptly stopped taking all the drugs and voluntarily re-entered rehab two weeks later.

24-Hour Experience

I began treatment again on November 12, 2002. On the first night, I remembered Jeremy Brown, who had told me that no matter what I had done, Christ loves me and is waiting for me to call out to Him in repentance and faith. It didn't happen in a church service, under a revival tent, or in a crusade. Jesus introduced Himself to me that night in my room. I surrendered myself to Him, confessing my sins and asking the Lord to save me from the mess I had made of my life. After dumping everything at the foot of the cross, God's forgiveness rushed over me like a mighty, cleansing wave. Overwhelmed by a purity and freedom I had never known, I made two promises to the Lord that night: first, I would completely devote my life to Him, and second, I would travel the world sharing my testimony with others.

I spent the next twenty-four hours in my room with nobody but Jesus Christ. This glorious experience birthed uncontainable excitement in my soul. The very next day, I told my dad that I intended to become a preacher. A lifelong Catholic, my father was concerned about my plans for marriage. Naturally, he assumed that I wanted to become a priest. I carefully explained that I was leaving my focus on rituals and works behind, and I was devoting my life to sharing the gospel with others.

Questions to Consider

Remember how you felt when you came to Christ. Did someone come alongside you to assist you in growing in your newfound faith? Was it even an option for you?

The Difference that Made the Difference

Making the transition from religion to a personal relationship with Christ was extremely difficult for me. My Catholic upbringing didn't promote Scripture reading, memorization, or unrehearsed prayer. For several months, I wandered aimlessly in my Christian life, uncertain of how to proceed.

Sensing my desperate frustration, a friend suggested that I pray for God to provide a mentor to disciple me, just as Paul had discipled Timothy. Because I had never read the Bible, I was unfamiliar with Paul and Timothy's relationship. But in spite of my nervous skepticism, I began to pray for God to send someone to help me.

I began attending Edgewater Baptist Church in New Orleans. After a few weeks, a church member by the name of David Platt invited me to meet weekly with him for Bible study, prayer, and accountability. When he asked me to pray about joining him, I excitedly responded, "I have already been praying. When do we start?"

I couldn't believe that God had heard my sincere plea for help, and had prompted David to offer to disciple me in the Christian life. For the next five months, I met with David every week to discuss the glory of God, the lost nature of man, and the good news of Christ. Throughout this time, David constantly encouraged me to share my story with others. The following month, I enrolled in New Orleans Baptist Theological Seminary to prepare for a lifetime of ministry. We continued meeting, enlarging our group to seven other seminary students, every Tuesday and Thursday mornings at six thirty for the next eighteen months.

Shortly after, God graciously brought another key person into my life. Tim LaFleur, a campus minister at Nicholls State University, invited me to work with him for the summer in Glorieta, New Mexico, helping hundreds of college students grow into mature followers of Christ. We spent those three months discussing the essential doctrines of the faith, the power of the Holy Spirit, the equipping of saints for service, and the assurance of salvation. He straightened out my faulty theology, always correcting me with grace and love.

In addition to David and Tim, a number of other selfless men invested themselves in discipling me. I am eternally grateful to Don Wilton, Tony Merida, Reggie Ogea, Larry Osborne, John Willoughby, Mark Dever, Bill Hull, and Bryant Wright as well. These men have been "Pauls" in my life, instructing and challenging me to do for others exactly what they did for me.

Question to Consider

For those of you who have been discipled, what are some ways you have benefited from discipleship?

Reality Check

Though my story sounds unique, I'm really not alone. We all come out of sin and into a relationship with Christ. *Everyone* needs to be discipled, regardless of their background. As I grew in my faith and knowledge of God's Word, I became aware that very few believers have had someone in their lives who accepted the responsibility of equipping them in the foundational doctrines, principles, and practices of the faith. In fact, I observed that most church members have yet to experience the benefits of personal discipleship.

Having surveyed churches for the past eighteen years, David Olson, director of the American Church Research Project, reported eye-opening results. He found that "on any given weekend in 1990, 20.4 percent of the American population attended an orthodox Christian church. On any given weekend in 2000, 18.7 percent of the American population attended an orthodox Christian church. In 2003, the Christian church attendance percentage was 17.8 percent. If the present rate of decline continues, in 2050, 11.7 percent of the population will be in a Christian church on any given weekend."[4] If the numbers drop as Olson projects, the future is bleak for the body of Christ in America.

T-NET International, a Colorado-based organization that trains and coaches pastors to fulfill the Great Commission, conducted a survey to determine if churches were producing disciples. Their team polled over 4,000 churchgoers from thirty-five churches representing different denominations. Bob Gilliam, co-founder and president of T-NET International, reported, "Many people in these churches are not growing spiritually. Of those taking this survey, 24 percent indicated that their behavior was sliding backward, and 41 percent said they were 'static' in their spiritual growth."[5] Thus, 65 percent of believers are either stalled or declining in their spiritual life.

Did you grasp the seriousness of these numbers? Six out of ten church attendees admitted that their spiritual lives were stagnant. Should the Christian life be stagnant? Is *static* a proper term to describe followers of Christ? Every single one of us should be closer to Christ today than we were a year ago, or even a month ago.

Wake Up Call

Five years after writing about mobilizing, inspiring and leading others, Bill Hybels, Senior Pastor of Willow Creek Community Church, publicly apologized to his congregation for failing to produce disciples in his church. Hybels hired a company to evaluate Willow Creek's effectiveness, and the results caused Hybels to experience the "wake-up call" of his ministerial life.[6] Acknowledging Willow Creek's failure, Hybels expressed his frustration. "We made a mistake. What we should have done when people crossed the line of faith and became Christians, we should have started telling people and teaching people that they have to take responsibility to become 'self-feeders.' We should have gotten people, taught people how to read their Bible between services, and how to do the spiritual practices much more aggressively on their own."[7]

After investing thirty years of ministry and tens of millions of dollars in facilities, programs, and promotions, Willow Creek was admittedly unsuccessful in producing disciples. Resources were prioritized on attracting visitors, but a step-by-step plan for personal growth was ignored.

How important is discipleship to pastors? In study after study, pastors have repeatedly ranked discipleship at the bottom of their priority list. The average church today focuses on programs and the public worship experience. Few have any real emphasis on personal discipleship, much less any structure or instruction for performing it.

Jason Mandryk of *Operation World* directly confronted this problem: "Discipleship is the greatest challenge facing the Church today. . . . There is a genuine need for effective Bible study and teaching in Christians' heart languages, genuine fellowship, and a commitment to involvement in ministry."[8]

It's Not All the Church's Fault

Speaking about the impact Christians have on the world, or the lack thereof, Greg Nettle stated, "The lack of discipleship undermines all else that we seek to do."[9] So who is to blame for this oversight? It is unfair to blame the church exclusively. While the shortcomings of the church in discipleship cannot be overlooked, it is also true that many professing Christians never commit to a growing relationship with the Lord.

In the Parable of the Sower, Jesus taught us that many who receive the Word of God never grow and bear fruit for Him. A shallow commitment and love for the things of this world—this life—stunt their growth as believers (Matt. 13:3–9, 18–23).

The fact is, nearly all evangelical churches emphasize, to some degree, Bible study and prayer, which are the basic keys to knowing God. Most offer some sort of Bible study or D-Groups (this concept will be explained in chapter 3), albeit, often ineffectively.

But, in the best of churches, only a fraction of the membership even attends a worship service regularly. Smaller still is the percentage of people who are faithfully involved in a group or class.

Jesus pulled no punches when it came to discipleship. He was blunt and crystal-clear about it: following Him is a choice, a choice that requires sacrifice, commitment, and making Him the number one priority of our lives. There is a price involved with being His disciple. He forewarned us, and many professing believers count the cost and decide it is more than they are willing to pay (Luke 14:26–33).

Questions to Consider

In your opinion, why hasn't discipleship been a priority for the church? Why hasn't it been a priority for you?

The Master's Model

As Jesus discipled the twelve men who would change the world, He gradually released them into ministry. The four-step progression He initiated applies to disciple-making today.

First, *Jesus ministered while the disciples watched.* In the Sermon on the Mount, Jesus taught God's truths, and the disciples observed, listened, and learned (Matt. 5–7). When Jesus went into the synagogue and healed the lame, cleansed the lepers, and gave hearing to the deaf, the disciples looked on (Mark 1:21–22).

Second, *Jesus progressed to allowing the disciples to assist him in ministry.* When Jesus fed the multitude,

He broke the bread and performed the miracle. The disciples distributed the supernatural meal to the hungry crowd, and they also collected the surplus (John 6:1–13).

Third, *the disciples ministered, and Jesus assisted them.* After His glorious transfiguration, Jesus came down from the mountain and walked into an uproar (Mark 9). The disciples were attempting to cast out a demon from a possessed boy, and they were failing miserably. In utter frustration and desperation, the boy's father turned to Jesus and asked Him to intervene. "I brought my son to your disciples, but they could do nothing!" the despondent man cried. Jesus stepped in, cast out the demon, and made the boy whole. Later, Jesus rebuked the powerless disciples, instructing them that *"this kind cannot be driven out by anything but prayer"* (Mark 9:29).

The final step of the disciples' training was *Jesus observing as the disciples ministered to others.* Jesus sent them out with the instruction to go into the world, cast out demons, and preach the gospel. And they came back saying, "Jesus, it was just like you said. We cast out demons and we preached the good news. God miraculously worked through us" (Luke 10:1–17).

This is the model Jesus gave us, and this is His plan for developing disciples today. You can't do this alone, and you shouldn't attempt to.

Question to Consider

*Consider Jesus's four-step process
for making disciples. Why is
it an effective strategy?*

Where Do I Begin?

In order to make disciples, we must first *be* disciples. In the average evangelical church, what happens immediately after someone comes to saving faith in Christ? Most ministers encourage the new believer to live for Christ, deny sin, and attend church faithfully. Completely puzzled, the baby believer leaves the service as clueless about following Christ as he or she was upon entering. Sadly, this scenario is repeated in many Bible-preaching churches every week. Sincere believers who desire a vibrant relationship with the Lord are sent out the doors totally unaware of how to cultivate intimacy with their Savior.

The words *spring cleaning* spark fear and dread in the minds of most children. If your parents were anything like mine, once a year they would rise early on a Saturday morning to reorganize the garage, basement, or storage shed behind the house. The first year I was old enough to assist, my hard work paid off. As I was moving lawn equipment and bicycles out of the way, a massive black box caught my attention from the back corner of our shed. After climbing over old mattresses and furniture to reach it, I carefully maneuvered my way out of the shed without dropping my newfound treasure. "What is it, Dad?" I excitedly asked.

My father bent down, wiped the dust off the black box, and with a smile on his face responded, "This is the world radio I had when I was your age." I was fascinated.

My dad and I spent the remainder of the day cleaning the radio rather than the garage. Later that night, our family gathered around that old radio, and, with fingers crossed, plugged the cord into the outlet. To everyone's happy surprise, it worked just as it had twenty years earlier. Although we could not hear or see the radio frequencies being transmitted through the air, stations from China, France, and Europe came in clearly with a careful turn of the dial.

As I think fondly back on that day, I am reminded that God speaks to us every day. But, in order to hear His voice, we must be tuned in to His frequency. As in human relationships, communication with God is the foundation of an intimate walk with Him. Yet, many believers never learn how to tune in to God. For them, hearing from God is an elusive concept.

Multiplication over Addition

Moreover, God has always been interested in reproduction. In fact, His first command to Adam and Eve in the Garden was not to be spiritual, productive, or upstanding citizens of earth. Rather, it was to *"be fruitful and multiply"* (Gen. 1:28). What God commanded the first humans to do physically is what Jesus commanded believers to do spiritually. The goal of every D-Group is for the mentee, the one being discipled, to become a mentor; to multiply—make other disciples.

In essence, the D-Group is designed for the player to become a coach. As the leader, you must communicate this purpose at the outset of the group. If it is not discussed early on, members in the group will adopt a consumer mentality, with a short-sighted, self-serving focus. The heart of discipleship, as Christ modeled and instituted it, is that you are not learning only for yourself. You are learning for the person whom you will mentor in following Him.

The Great Commission is designed to be a team effort. Instead of the pastors/leaders/Sunday school teachers/deacons performing all the duties of ministry in the church, the saints are equipped to carry out the work. The ministers cannot carry out the command alone, as Paul clearly stated:

And he gave the apostles, the prophets, the evan-
gelists, the shepherds and teachers, to equip the
saints for the work of ministry. (Eph. 4:11–12)

Greg Ogden, in his book *Transforming Discipleship*, expounds on this point by graphically illustrating the contrast between someone personally seeing one person come to the Lord every day for a year, as compared to investing in the same two people for an entire year (see Figure 1). The evangelist hits the streets every day with the goal of sharing the gospel with as many people as needed to see God save one person. In contrast, the disciple-maker walks two people through a year of intensive discipleship.

The slow-moving discipleship process creeps forward with only four people being impacted in two years, compared to 730 converts through the solitary work of a busy evangelist. However, this radically changes with the passing of time. After sixteen years of the same activity, the evangelist would have seen almost 6,000 people come to faith in Christ, while the disciple would have impacted 65,536 people. Every person on the planet would be reached multiple times over after thirty years. It is a ministry shift from a strategy of addition, where the clergy performs the ministerial duties, to one of multiplication, where believers are expected and equipped to personally participate in the Great Commission.

Multiplication—not addition—is Jesus's plan for reaching the world with the gospel. And multiplication is the purpose of the D-Group. If the body of Christ would accept this plan, embrace it, and faithfully obey it, then the Great Commission would be accomplished.

Evangelistic Addition vs Disciplemaking Multiplication			
Year	Evangelist	Discipler	D-Group of 3
1	365	2	3
2	730	4	9
3	1,095	8	27
4	1,460	16	81
5	1,825	32	243
6	2,190	64	729
7	2,555	128	2,187
8	2,920	256	6,561
9	3,285	512	19,683
10	3,650	1,024	59,049
11	4,015	2,048	177,147
12	4,380	4,096	531,441
13	4,745	8,192	1,594,323
14	5,110	16,384	4,782,969
15	5,475	32,768	14,348,907
16	5,840	65,536	43,046,721

Figure 1[10]

Nothing Grows under a Banyan Tree

The banyan is a massive tree that develops secondary trunks to support its enormous branches. A full-grown banyan tree can cover an entire acre. The tree provides shade and shelter for many animals with its branches, but nothing is able to grow under its dense foliage. Therefore, the earth beneath it is barren.

A banana tree is exactly the opposite. Within six months, small shoots sprout from the ground. Six months later, another set of shoots spring from the earth to join the others, which are now six months old. After about eighteen months, bananas burst forth from the main trunk of the tree. Humans, birds, and many other creatures benefit from its fruit before it dies. Every six months, the cycle is reproduced, with sprouts forming, fruit bearing, and shoots dying. The end result is a forest of banana trees.

These contrasting trees graphically illustrate a vital discipleship truth. Many people practice a banyan style of leadership. Mitsuo Fukuda explained, "Banyan-style leaders have a tremendous ministry, but have difficulty finding a successor, because they do not generate leaders, only followers. It's possible to grow followers in a relatively short space of time, and that's a useful result in its own. But when the leader goes away, you are left only with a heavily dependent group of people, programmed with a list of instructions."[11]

Discipleship is about shoots and sprouts. These new sprouts are never a threat to the banana tree, for they ensure growth. In fact, they are expected. The goal of a D-Group is for the mentee to become a mentor, for the player to become a coach. Unless that happens, the group never progresses beyond a small group Bible study.

Points to Ponder

What style of ministry have you embraced? Are you consuming ministry, or are you creating ministry?

Memory Verse
Matthew 28:18–20

Chapter 2

THE GREAT CONFUSION

"Go therefore and make disciples of all nations,
baptizing them in the name of the Father and
of the Son and of the Holy Spirit, teaching them
to observe all that I have commanded you."
Matthew 28:19–20

"The subject of Discipleship is frequently discussed
today. Men are called to become disciples without
any definition of the concept, and without any clari-
fication of the requirements the Lord makes of those
who are His disciples. Hence no intelligent decision
can be made concerning this important question."
J. Dwight Pentecost

Imagine that, out of the blue, you receive a phone call
from a friend asking you to come to his house immediately. When you get there, he begins with these words:
"I am about to entrust you with information that will
save millions of lives and change the course of history.
However, there is only one stipulation: you must take
it to the world."

After affirming your commitment to follow through with his request, he proceeds to tell you something incredible: he has found the cure for cancer.

How will you broadcast this life-saving remedy? That night you would call every newspaper and news channel available to report the story. Appearances on talk shows and television programs would fill your calendar. Every time you communicated with the outside world, you would share information about this new-found discovery.

Two thousand years ago, the Creator of the universe wrapped Himself in human flesh and came to earth on a mission to redeem mankind. He did not come with the cure for cancer, AIDS, or any other life-threatening illness. He came with the remedy for our greatest problem: His sacrifice on the cross would cure the soul-destroying cancer of sin.

How would the Lord spread the greatest news in the world? He could write it in the clouds or announce it from heaven. He could employ all of His supernatural powers to instantly transmit this crucial message across the face of the earth.

But He didn't do that.

In His infinite wisdom, Jesus entrusted the message of redemption to twelve ordinary men. He chose to leave the mission of taking the gospel to the world in the hands of His disciples, men in whom He had personally invested.

Jesus's final words became the first priority of these men's lives. In Matthew 28:18, the Lord announced His supreme authority over heaven and earth. Then, He directed His followers, *"Go therefore and make disciples of all nations, baptizing them in the name of the Father and of the Son and of the Holy Spirit"* (Matt. 28:19).

Feel the weight of these words. This is not a sugges-
tion, an option, or even a choice for those who decide
to follow Jesus. Jesus extended this mandate to every
believer from every tongue, tribe, and nation: *"Go and
make disciples."*

This solemn charge is generally referred to as the
"Great Commission." In *Gospel Centered Discipleship,*
author Jonathan Dodson labels it the "Gospel
Commission" and highlights its three important
aspects:

- *Go*—this is the missional (missionary) aspect.
  Every believer is to participate in taking the
  gospel to others.
- *Baptize*—this is the relational (family) aspect.
  Every believer should instruct all who believe
  upon Christ to announce their relationship
  with Him and His people through the sym-
  bolic act of baptism.
- *Teach*—this is the rational (learner) aspect.
  Every believer is to teach others about Jesus
  and how to follow Him.[12]

Going, baptizing, and *teaching* define Jesus's prescribed method for making disciples. Picture these
terms as legs supporting the seat of a stool. Without
them, you are unsteady. With them, you are seated on
a firm foundation.

In order to fully carry out the command of the Great
Commission, we must understand a crucial term in this
verse. The King James Version of the Bible renders the
Greek word for *make disciples* as *teach.* Matthew 28:19
in the King James Version reads, *"Go ye therefore, and
teach all nations . . ."* (emphasis mine).

Many diligent believers simply read this word and
merely *teach* people about salvation—share the gospel,

and lead them to a decision for Christ. This is good and admirable, but it is not what Jesus asked. More is required to make a disciple of Jesus Christ. It is only one aspect of Jesus's command. Making disciples requires equipping, training, and investing in new believers.

So what is disciple-making? We could say that it is *intentionally equipping believers with the Word of God through accountable relationships empowered by the Holy Spirit in order to replicate faithful followers of Christ.* When people become disciples, they learn what Jesus said and live out what Jesus did (Matt. 28:19).

Questions to Consider

What are the three aspects of the Great Commission? Are you engaged in all three?

Be a Disciple

Disciple-making was a priority for Jesus and His disciples, and it should be a priority for us now. Bill Hull, a leader in personally obeying the Great Commission, has sounded the clarion call for discipleship over the past twenty years. He rightly insists that understanding "what a disciple is and what a disciple does are top priorities for the church."[13] He notes that many churches are carelessly guilty of throwing "the word disciple around freely, but too often with no definition."[14]

Perhaps the most common term used by believers in our day is the word *Christian.* But do you know how many times *Christian* appears in the Bible? Only three times (Acts 11:26; Acts 26:28; 1 Pet. 4:16). In its two occurrences in Acts, which present the history of the term, it is used as a derogatory slur. In fact, *Christian* was likely coined as a term of derision. Those who despised Christ displayed their disgust for His followers by calling them "Little Christs." It wasn't until years after Christ's ascension that the term was used in a positive light.

On the other hand, the term *disciple* appears 269 times in the New Testament, with 238 of those occurring in the four Gospels (the root word is used 281 times in the New Testament and 250 times in the Gospels alone). Why is this so important?

The answer is because Christ did not come to make *Christians*; He came to make *disciples*. Immediately before leaving this world to return to heaven, He commanded us—His disciples—to carry on that work in His absence. But before a person can make disciples, he or she must first *be* a disciple.

What does it mean to be a disciple? At the very core, a disciple is a learner, one who is set on growing and developing. In nearly every sphere of life, people learn specific skills from someone else who has developed those skills. An electrical certification is attained only after an extensive apprenticeship with a more experienced electrician. When a prospective doctor finishes medical school, she invests several years in a residency, a time of shadowing an experienced physician.

If a psychiatrist bases his practice on the teachings of Sigmund Freud, we might say he is a disciple of Freud. If a musician, following the methods of Wynton Marsalis, plays jazz in the same style, we might comment that he is a disciple of Wynton Marsalis. This concept of learning directly through the expertise and experience of another is the foundation of what Jesus envisioned when He used the term *disciple."*

Questions to Consider

What is the distinction between being a disciple and being a Christian? Would you consider yourself to be a disciple?

Confusion Over the Terms

Surprisingly, not everyone who talks about discipleship actually practices it. One reason for the misunderstanding is the ambiguity of what the word actually means. Boyd Luter Jr. addressed the misconceptions of many about what *discipleship* is: "Many Christian workers view discipleship as an activity that is to take place apart from the local church and that has little relationship to the church's major purpose."[15]

Similarly, many churches perpetuate this misunderstanding. They view discipleship as merely one segment of what the church offers. Discipleship, or disciple-making, should not be just another option, Bible study, or box to check on the church's program list. It should be the outflow of meaningful relationships built within the course of daily life, including at church, work, and in neighborhood contacts. Discipleship is a way of life. It is the practice Jesus's Church is based on. Mike Breen and Steve Cockram, in *Building a Discipling Culture*, wrote, "If you make disciples, you always get the Church. But if you make a Church, you rarely get disciples."[16]

Another reason for the lack of disciple-making is the influence of the secular world upon believers. As

Christians, we can easily fall into the trap of gauging success in the church by our buildings, the number of bodies present, and the size of our budgets. However, this mentality presents a serious problem: Jesus never gauged effectiveness by these criteria. During His earthly ministry, He never owned anything. In fact, our Lord never had a place to lay His head, much less a regular meeting place for His "congregation" (Luke 9:58).

Additionally, Jesus never attempted to draw large crowds for the sake of counting heads. Although He spoke to the masses, He consistently departed to be with the twelve.[17] Acts 1 records that, after He ascended into heaven, only 120 disciples gathered together to pray for God to empower them through the sending of His Spirit. This fact defies all modern church growth standards. Jesus spoke with unprecedented authority. He raised the dead. He gave sight to the blind. He healed the sick.

And yet, at the end of His ministry, the church had grown to only 120 people. This is not to discount the miraculous work of our Lord, but to simply point out that Jesus was not interested in growing a mile wide and an inch deep. Rather, He focused on developing mature, faithful disciples who would go out and make more disciples.

Finally, Jesus was not impressed with finances. It's true that He taught on money more than heaven and hell combined, but He never put much stock in the size of the traveling treasury. Consider whom He put in charge of His ministry funds: Judas, who betrayed Him for a meager thirty pieces of silver.

Jesus, as demonstrated above, measured success by something other than buildings, bodies, and bucks.[18] He taught us that disciple-making is what matters, and it is a process that takes time. Remember, you can't microwave disciples.

Unfortunately, many have never been discipled by someone. Once again, Mike Breen is helpful in highlighting the disconnect found in most churches: "Maybe you've grown up in church. Maybe you've even gone to seminary. Maybe you lead a church, small group or Bible study. Maybe you've read every Christian book there is to read from the last 50 years. Great! It means you have an outstanding informational foundation. But you still might need to be discipled in the way that the Bible understands discipleship."[19]

Could it be that believers minimize discipleship in the church because they never had the privilege of being discipled? It is difficult—nearly impossible—to lead someone on a journey you have never been on. Whom can you ask to invest what they have learned about following Christ into your life?

Question to Consider

*How have you gauged
success in a church?*

First Things First

Imagine that you were present in Jerusalem on the Day of Pentecost when Peter, empowered by the Holy Spirit, preached, and 3,000 people responded to the gospel. If you were one of the apostles, what would you do next? Would you count hands and heads? Have them each fill out a card? Report the numbers to the denomination?

No, not if you were one of these twelve. The apostles had one agenda: to make disciples who make disciples. They went to the drawing board to construct a plan to disciple each and every person. Their only goal was to develop each of the 3,000 new believers into a fully devoted follower of Jesus, one who would make additional disciples of others.

Similarly, Paul sketched out the same roadmap to Timothy in his final letter to his son in the faith: *"You then, my child, be strengthened by the grace that is in Christ Jesus, and what you have heard from me in the presence of many witnesses entrust to faithful men who will be able to teach others also"* (2 Tim. 2:1–2). This single verse describes four generations of discipleship. Paul discipled Timothy. Timothy discipled faithful men. And these men, in turn, discipled others (five generations are present if you consider Jesus's investment in Paul). Billy Graham claimed this verse had a greater impact on his view of discipleship than any other in the Bible:

> One of the first verses of scripture that Dawson Trotman, the founder of Navigators, called me to memorize was 2 Timothy 2:2. He said, "This is like a mathematical formula for spreading the gospel and enlarging the church. Paul taught Timothy. Timothy shared what he knew with faithful men. And the faithful men were supposed to teach others also. And so the process goes on. If every believer followed this pattern, the church could reach the entire world in one generation." If the church followed this pattern, we could reach the world in one generation. Mass crusades in which I believe and to which I have committed my life will never

accomplish the Great Commission; one-on-one relationships will.[20]

Many Christians are birthed into the family of God and then abandoned. Nobody personally assumes the responsibility of helping them develop and grow. Nobody teaches them the basics of the Christian life, disciplines like Bible reading, prayer, Scripture memory, meditation, sharing one's faith, or showing the love of Christ to others. Indeed, in many churches, the only discipleship offered is from the pulpit on Sunday.

Does Preaching Produce Disciples?

Unfortunately, preaching alone will not produce disciples. Several years ago, I emailed disciple-maker Avery Willis, creator of Masterlife, inquiring about the role of preaching in making disciples. He graciously replied, "I really don't believe much discipling is done through preaching, Robby. Yes, you can impart information and emotion in preaching, but discipleship is more relational, more one on one . . . preaching to make disciples is like going to the nursery and spraying the crying babies with milk and saying that you just fed the kids." He went on to say, "I am not against preaching; I do it all the time. But Jesus chose twelve and lived with them, explained to them, gave them assignments, debriefed them . . . to shape and mold them to be like Him. His sermons no doubt helped convey the truth, but He had to follow up most of it with what I call *discipling*."[21]

Do not misunderstand me. I am not minimizing the importance of preaching. I have devoted my life to it. However, discipleship involves more than preaching and listening. It integrates intimate, accountable relationships that are rooted in the Word of God, which cultivates enduring, fruitful lives.

After surveying the preaching in the New Testament, observing the practices of great preachers, and considering modern ministries today, Peter Adam came to this same realization. He determined that "while preaching . . . is one form of the ministry of the Word, many other forms are reflected in the Bible and in contemporary Christian church life. It is important to grasp this point clearly, or we shall try and make preaching carry a load which it cannot bear, that is, the burden of doing all that the Bible expects of every form of ministry of the Word."[22]

The Great Confusion

My wife, Kandi, called me one morning to see if I had lunch plans. While I was checking my schedule, a staff member entered my office needing counsel on a pressing issue. I inattentively replied to my wife, "I would love to go to lunch. Where do you want to go?" She mentioned the name of the restaurant at the same time my co-worker asked me a question. My last words to her were, "I'll see you in ten minutes."

When I pulled into the parking lot of the restaurant, her car was nowhere in sight. Five minutes went by, then ten. Concerned, I dialed her cell phone and asked, "Baby, where are you?"

She responded, "In the parking lot; where are you?" I jumped out of my truck with my phone in hand and searched the lot thoroughly, but I could not spot her. Then it dawned on me. I traveled to the right restaurant, but to the wrong location.

Have you ever listened to someone speak without hearing what they are saying? We men are notorious for this. We may even nod our heads in agreement with our wives as they ask us to take out the garbage, cut the grass, or carry the laundry to the laundry room, but we rarely follow up on their requests. Similarly, I wonder what God thinks about believers who read the Great Commission in Matthew 28:18–20, hear sermons that emphasize the importance of the Great Commission, are challenged to follow through with going and making disciples, and even affirm the pastor as he preaches on discipleship, but never act upon what Jesus actually told them.

Many believers "pass the buck" by delegating their God-assigned task of making disciples to the pastors or other trained leaders of the church. The command of Jesus is crystal-clear. Yet many believers and churches fall far short of following Jesus's irrefutable priority for our lives and ministries.

Question to Consider

What are some steps your church needs to take to become a disciple-making church?

Ministry Myths

Steve Murrell, in his book *WikiChurch*, identified three myths that hinder disciple-making today: the mentoring myth, the ministry myth, and the maturity myth.[23] The mentoring myth cripples believers into thinking that only vocational ministers should do the work of the ministry.

When Mr. Jimmy, a friend and elderly church member, was admitted into the hospital for a back procedure, I had prayer with him at the hospital before his surgery. Two weeks later, someone stopped me after the Sunday service with these words: "Mr. Jimmy is upset with you because no one visited him since his procedure." Surprised, I replied, "That's just not true. Three people visited him over the past two weeks." The day after the surgery, my associate pastor spent time at the hospital with him. Later that week, a deacon visited him, and the following week, another deacon spent the afternoon with him.

I stopped by his house after church to get to the bottom of the misunderstanding. As I walked in the door, I asked, "Mr. Jimmy, how are you doing?" "Not good," answered Mr. Jimmy. "Not good, preacher." Puzzled, I asked, "Why is that?" He proceeded to explain the source of his discouragement: he had not been visited since his surgery. I lovingly corrected his confusion by highlighting the fact that Jonathan, my associate pastor, saw him in the hospital, Todd visited later that week, and Ted stopped by his home prior to Sunday's service. He replied, "No, Pastor, *you* didn't visit me."

This manner of thinking, prominent in many churches today, is what Larry Osborne labeled the Holy Man Myth. "The Holy Man Myth," observed Osborne, "is the idea that pastors and clergy somehow have a more direct line to God. It cripples a church because it overburdens pastors and underutilizes the gifts and anointing of everyone else. It mistakenly equates leadership gifts with superior spirituality."[24] Left uncorrected, this myth will paralyze people in the pews.

The second myth common in most churches is the ministry myth. Those plagued by this view will say, "Because of my previous sins, my reserved personality, my lack of talents, or my laziness to read the

Word, pray, or memorize Scripture, I am not ready for ministry."

The final myth is the maturity myth, which suggests that full Christian growth must be achieved before ministry can be performed. Many have said, "I will be ready for ministry after I go to seminary," or, "When I complete another Bible study, I should be prepared," or, "As soon as I receive this diploma, ask me to serve." Fearful that someone may ask them a question for which they have no answer, these individuals idly sit by without ever participating in any ministry. In so doing, they fail to achieve their purpose as a Christian and forfeit God's blessing upon their lives.

Mythbusters

Paul clearly and completely debunked these myths in his letter to the church at Ephesus:

> [11]*And he gave the apostles, the prophets, the evangelists, the shepherds and teachers,* [12]*to equip the saints for the work of ministry, for building up the body of Christ,* [13]*until we all attain to the unity of the faith and of the knowledge of the Son of God, to mature manhood, to the measure of the stature of the fullness of Christ.* (Eph. 4:11–13)

Notice the progression of this text. In verse 11, Paul identified the mentors. In verse 12, he outlined the ministry. And in verse 13, he expressed the maturity of believers. Most churches incorrectly reorganize the text in this manner: verse 11, verse 13, and then verse 12.[25] Discouraged pastors/mentors/leaders passively wait for members to mature by attending Sunday school, Bible studies, conferences, seminaries, or church for an extended period of time before asking them to participate in service. Somehow, we have equated degrees, diplomas, and attendance pins with maturity.

If we simply follow the intentional flow of this text, we will see the Scriptural model for disciple-making. *Ministry is the pathway to maturity*, not the other way around. The job of pastors, mentors, and leaders is to equip believers to carry out their God-given ministry. Their effectiveness is not gauged by their performance of ministerial duties alone, but by their development of other disciples, preachers, pastors, godly fathers, and Christ-honoring students (v. 11).

Second, a proper understanding of verse 12 destroys the "ministry myth." Regardless of whether people are bold or shy, God can and will use them. Even if a believer doesn't pray like they should, read the Bible enough, or possess all the skills needed to answer every question asked, they can still be involved in ministry (v. 12). Every believer is commanded to make disciples. There are no courses to take, no tests to pass, and no hoops to jump through first.

Finally, this text proves that maturity happens through ministry, not vice versa (v. 13). The demands of ministry cannot wait until believers feel mature enough to minister. Jesus's (and Paul's) expectation was for every believer to make disciples—not some, not many, not most, but *all* believers. Being a Christian and making disciples are inseparable. Dietrich Bonheoffer, a German theologian and pastor who laid down his life for the gospel, recorded the same sentiment in his classic, *The Cost of Discipleship.* He wrote, "Christianity without the living Christ is inevitably Christianity without discipleship, and Christianity without discipleship is always Christianity without Christ."[26] Discipleship is not only basic training for battle; it is the hospital for healing and recovering.

Three Indispensable Relationships

Howard Hendricks, beloved professor at Dallas Theological Seminary who went to be with the Lord in 2013, taught that every believer should foster three relationships in their life:

- A *Paul*—an older and wiser believer from whom you can learn
- A *Barnabas*—a friend who teaches, encourages, and holds you accountable
- A *Timothy*—a young believer [believers] in whom you are investing[27]

These three relationships allow others to speak into your life, and, at the same time, allow you to speak into others' lives. Notice the wisdom of Solomon: *"Iron sharpens iron, and one man sharpens another"* (Prov. 27:17).

Questions to Consider

Can you identify each of the three relationships in your life: Paul, Barnabas, and Timothy? If not, who are potential individuals who could fill these roles?

Now What?

Although George Martin challenged pastors to think about their ministry with the end in mind, his comments are applicable to every believer:

Perhaps today's pastor should imagine that they are going to have three more years in their parish (church) as pastor—that there will be no replacement for them when they leave. If they acted as if this were going to happen, they would put the highest priority on selecting, motivating, and training lay leaders that could carry on as much as possible the mission of the parish after they left. The results of three sustained years of such an approach would be significant. Even revolutionary.[28]

If you knew that the time clock of your life expired three years from today, how would you live? Would you change anything? What steps would you take to leave a lasting legacy, an eternal impact? You wouldn't neglect discipling your children, family, and friends if you only had three years left with them.

Of all the options Jesus had to spread the greatest message in the world, the redemption of humankind through His sacrifice, He chose to entrust it to twelve men. Ultimately, through the passing of the centuries, it has been entrusted to us. We are the current link in the chain described in 2 Timothy 2:2. Shouldn't we live with the same urgency?

Every believer should be able to answer two questions. Who am I discipling? And who is discipling me? Every church should be able to answer two questions. Do we have a plan for making disciples? And is it working?

Question to Consider

If you only had three years left to live, who would you invest in? How would you prioritize your time?

Memory Verse
2 Timothy 2:1–2

Chapter 3

THE D-GROUP:
A BLUEPRINT

"Go therefore and make disciples of all nations,
baptizing them in the name of the Father
and of the Son and of the Holy Spirit."
Matthew 28:19

"One must decide if he wants his ministry to
count in momentary applause of popular recogni-
tion or the reproduction of his life in a few chosen
men to carry on his work after he has gone."
Robert Coleman

"Make disciples!"
Two thousand years ago, this command rang
through the Galilean countryside and into the ears
of Jesus's chosen twelve. These words, Jesus's final
words to His students, are commonly referred to as
the Great Commission. Its thrust is a heart-stirring
truth: God has chosen to reach all nations with the
gospel message by working through us. The Creator
and Redeemer has graciously made us His partners in
the eternally-crucial work of transforming hell-bound

sinners into heaven-bound students of Christ. As Paul explained to the carnal Corinthians, *"We are God's fellow workers"* (1 Cor. 3:9).

Luke recorded, both in his Gospel and in Acts, that Jesus promised His disciples that the Holy Spirit would come and empower them for the task (Luke 24:49; Acts 1:8). The faithful physician also encouraged us by relating that Jesus blessed them—and us—as He was carried away into heaven (Luke 24:50–51). Later, Paul informed us that when Jesus ascended into heaven, He gave them *gifts*—spiritually-imparted abilities—sufficient to accomplish the task (Eph. 4:8–16).

While for some it is merely an excuse for disobedience to the Lord's command, many believers genuinely feel unqualified and insufficient to participate in the work of making disciples. But Jesus did not command His disciples—and all of us who come behind them— to reach the world, then suddenly depart and leave us to our own resources. He fully equipped us with everything we need to get the job done: His Spirit, who dwells within us, and His blessing upon our efforts.

The driving purpose of this book is to help you become a disciple who makes disciples. In my experience—both in my personal, spiritual growth and in my ministry— the D-Group is the most effective vehicle for getting you to this destination. I am convinced that those who are serious about discipleship will be a part of a D-Group, and that churches that are serious about making disciples will both provide and promote D-Groups in the assembly.

WikiGroups

Have you heard of the online encyclopedia, Nupedia? Probably not.

Conceived in 2000 by Jimmy Wales and Larry Sanger, its goal was simple: contract the best and brightest doctors, historians, and professors from around the world to research and write scholarly articles which, upon completion, would be filtered through an extensive editing process and then uploaded to an online database. Due to the nature of the task, the project was extremely slow, causing the two owners to unplug the servers after three years with only twenty-four articles posted to the web and seventy-four others in the review stage.[29]

In 2001, Wales and Sanger launched a second project with the purpose of creating a feeder system for Nupedia. This subsequent venture adopted a different strategy. Average, ordinary men and women were encouraged to submit articles to the same editorial staff. For example, an avid golfer could submit an article about golf. Likewise, a football fan could write an article about his favorite team with stats, schedule, names of players, and coaches.

By the end of its first year, volunteers had submitted 20,000 "wiki" articles for consideration. At the time of this writing, eleven years later, what became known as Wikipedia is the largest encyclopedia on the Internet, boasting over 6 million articles in English alone, and more than 56 million articles across its 323 language editions.

How did they do it? Ordinary individuals were entrusted with the task of researching, compiling, and submitting articles pertaining to topics they were passionate about.

I am not suggesting that Wikipedia is completely accurate or reliable. I simply want you to notice how volunteers created the most widely accessible encyclopedia on the planet.

Tragically for souls and the cause of Christ, many churches and ministries operate under the Nupedia model, rather than the Wikipedia model. Only the accredited, professional believers are enlisted to lead D-Groups or mission efforts, while the rest of the members sit by idly watching others do what God has commissioned *them* to do. Steve Murrell in *WikiChurch* offered a challenge: "Imagine if the situation were reversed. Imagine if every believer, not just paid leaders, were engaged in ministry. That's a WikiChurch. That's the book of Acts."[30]

Bill Hull once spoke to my church after one of our discipleship enrichment weekend conferences. He began his message by sharing about the class he was teaching at Biola University in Southern California. On the first day of class, Bill outlined the plan for the next fifteen weeks to the students. "After every class," instructed Bill, "you will find one person to teach everything you learn from me each week. This will continue for the entire semester."

Curiosity painted the faces of all in attendance.

Bill continued, "At the end of the semester, that person will come to class and take the final exam for you. Your grade depends upon how well you invest what you learn in another person."[31] Would you have passed this class?

How many people have you personally discipled who are now repeating the process in others? When the church becomes an end in itself, it ends. When Sunday school, as great as it is, becomes an end in itself, it ends. When small groups ministry becomes an end in itself, it ends. When the worship service becomes an end in itself, it ends. What we need is for discipleship to become the goal, and then the process never ends. The process is fluid. It is moving. It is active. It is a living thing. It must continue to go on. Every disciple must make disciples.

Every Christian could be compared to one of two bodies of water: the Jordan River, or the Dead Sea. The Jordan River is an active body of water, flowing from north to south. The Dead Sea, on the other hand, has no outlets. Water comes in from the north to the lowest point in the world, and it doesn't flow back out. So the water is stagnant; it just sits there. I believe that every Christian is like one of these bodies of water. You are either flowing as God uses you to impact the lives of other people, or you are stagnant and lifeless, like the Dead Sea.

Question to Consider

Does your church reflect a Nupedia model, or a Wikipedia model?

Discipleship in Action

I am often asked, "What is the difference between a D-Group and a Sunday school class or a small group Bible study?" Allow me to reveal some of these differences.

First, the D-Group is a closed group, rather than an open group. Sunday school classes and Bible studies are usually open groups (or they should be); that is, they are open to anyone and everyone who would like to attend. A D-Group is, by design, closed to a handful of people. A person joins the group by invitation only.

Second, the purpose of a D-Group is completely different. While Sunday school classes and Bible studies exist for the purposes of growth and fellowship, they have an underlying additional purpose (or they should): evangelism. Sunday school classes are designed to reach lost people by getting them involved in the group. A D-Group, in contrast, consists of believers who desire a deeper walk with Christ. It is not evangelistic in its form or function, but in its fruit: it makes disciples, who then make disciples.

Lastly, the setting of the D-Group is completely different. It is the shift from a lecture, where one person teaches a room full of students, to an intimate, accountable relationship with a handful of like-minded people. In their book *The Invested Life*, Joel Rosenberg and T. E. Koshy suggest that a discipleship relationship is "more personal, more practical, and more powerful. While teacher shares information, a discipler shares life. A teacher aims for the head; while a discipler aims for the heart. A teacher measures knowledge; a discipler measures faith. A teacher is an authority; a discipler is a servant. A teacher says, 'Listen to me,' while a discipler says, 'Follow me.'"[32] This blueprint, sketched by Jesus Christ through His personal example, is how discipleship is accomplished in the lives of believers, and, ultimately, within the local church. When this plan is followed, those involved will participate in three dynamics that result in growth in their personal lives, as well as in the Kingdom: community and accountability.

If you'd like a plan for how to get D-Groups started in your church, check out www.replicate.org/dgroup.

Questions to Consider

*Have you ever confused a D-Group
with a small group or Bible study? If
so, list some ways in which you did?
How are the two groups different?*

Unity in the Community

John Wesley clearly understood that the only way
new believers' lives can be genuinely changed is by
creating a community around them where their new
beliefs can be practiced, expressed, and nurtured.[33] New
Testament believers, according to the account in Acts,
not only cared for one another, but *"devoted themselves
to the apostles' teaching and fellowship, to the breaking
of bread, and the prayers . . . [They] were together and
held all things in common"* (Acts 2:42–44). Believers
in the first church gathered, worshipped, worked,
and lived within the context of a family bond—one of
the hallmarks of disciple-making. This intimate relationship was driven by a common, unwavering belief
in the gospel of Jesus Christ. As they lived, labored,
and learned together, the Spirit of Jesus was in their
midst (Matt. 18:20). We too will find that, as we com-
mune with other believers, we will enjoy the presence
of Christ in a deeper, more vibrant manner.

Community is often synonymous with the word *fellowship,* or *koinonia* in the Greek language. Community
is developed when men and women unite around a
common interest; in this case, the gospel. Think of it
as people working in unity together. Fellowship can

be accurately defined as "two fellows in the same ship." Jesus taught us that genuine fellowship with other believers can be stronger and deeper than the blood relationships of father, mother, brother, or sister (Matt. 12:46–50). The preservation and protection of the *koinonia* within a local church, the ultimate symbol of discipleship (John 13:34–35), is not fortified by human enterprise or man-made initiatives; it is fashioned by the Holy Spirit (Phil. 2:1–2).

Community should include people at different stages in their journey of faith. Jesus demonstrated different levels of community in His discipleship model. From the larger community of Jews, He called twelve disciples, His own small group, to live with Him. From that group, He selected three, Peter, James, and John, for intimate training and a deeper relationship than the rest of the disciples.

Community also distributes the trust of the gospel to a greater pool of people. Throughout his epistles, Paul mentions a number of individuals who co-labored with him for the gospel's sake. Most were faithful, but some were not. Yet, the work continued, because the success of the mission did not depend on any one person's faithfulness.

The Necessity of Accountability

Life's journey is a winding road of twists and turns, sins, setbacks, and shortcomings. We are commanded by Paul to *"bear one another's burdens and so fulfill the law of Christ"* (Gal. 6:2). On one occasion, Jesus sent the disciples out to minister, and, upon their return, *"The apostles . . . told him all that they had done and taught"* (Mark 6:30). He not only delegated tasks to them, but He requested a report on how the mission went.

Chuck Swindoll described accountability as "opening one's life to a few carefully selected, trusted, loyal confidants who speak the truth—who have the right to examine, to question, to approve, and to give counsel."[34] Every believer is accountable to God (Heb. 9:27), to spiritual leaders (Heb. 13:17), and to other believers (Prov. 27:17). As the Holy Spirit enables us to pursue holiness, accountable relationships become the lifeblood for personal growth.

Accountability is not about condemning or criticizing; it is a tool we use to redeem and reconcile us back to Christ through a proper understanding of our identity as sons and daughters of God. We can accelerate our personal development through accountability questions: How is your relationship with your spouse? Is there any unconfessed sin in your life? Have you been modeling the gospel for your children? Are you reading the Bible each day?

Accountability best operates in the small setting of the D-Group. With introverts, a larger group often encourages shyness. A larger group also increases the risk of somebody abusing the accountability relationship by sharing confidential information, thereby harming a believer who stumbles. We will discuss confidentiality later, but allow me to park here for a minute. Woe to the man or woman who would break the confidentiality of an accountability relationship. A person who would carelessly spread the struggles of a growing child of God will surely face the severe judgment of the God who commanded us to *"confess [our] sins to one another and pray for one another, that (we) may be healed"* (James 5:16).

At this point, you may be thinking, "I will be accountable to no one." That, however, is not the case. Everyone is accountable to someone, in some form or fashion. Every role—citizen, spouse, child, employee, leader, follower—involves accountability on some level.

A wise person builds accountability into every relationship. The person who thinks he or she does not need to be accountable to anyone is a fool . . . and usually has something to hide.

It has been often said that your true character is revealed by what you would do if you had an absolute guarantee that nobody would ever find out. If that is true, most of us are probably sorely deficient of character! Accountability forces us to be at our best. When you spot a policeman, with radar gun in hand, you are likely to slow down and travel at the speed limit. When friends are coming for dinner, you clean up your house. If you are called upon to teach a small group lesson, you will study your Bible in preparation. You produce better work when you are supervised. You will be more careful on the Internet when someone else is reading your browser history. How many students would learn the material if they were never tested on it?

The hard truth is, the management of our sinful nature demands accountability. If you really understand this concept, then you must lower your guard and allow others into your life through transparency and honesty. *"The sin which clings so closely"* (Heb. 12:1) is more successfully overcome with the help of brothers or sisters to whom we are accountable. The spiritual disciplines essential to growth—Scripture reading and memory, prayer, obedience, to name a few—are nurtured through open, vulnerable discipleship relationships with other believers. Faithfulness to God's Word is cultivated through probing questions that go deeper than superficial conversation (See Appendix 7 for a list of accountability questions). The believer who is serious about walking faithfully with the Lord *will* make himself or herself accountable to others.

The accountability relationship is serious and sacred. Therefore, boundaries must be established at the outset of the discipling relationship in three areas: confidentiality, confrontation, and confession. A quick word of caution: you must wisely discern to whom you will make yourself accountable, carefully guarding whom you allow to speak into your life. Never seek spiritual guidance from unspiritual people.

Questions to Consider

Why is accountability important?
Name people that you have been
accountable to in the past? To whom
are you currently accountable?

Accountability Requires Confidentiality

Because of the sensitive information discussed during the meetings of a D-Group, everything needs to be confidential. When believers in a D-Group obey the command of Scripture to unload their problems onto other brothers or sisters in Christ, they do so knowing those in their group aren't going to use it as fodder for gossip. As genuine believers, we must be trustworthy in this area. Awareness of deep-seated sins in others' lives is a holy stewardship. No single action will destroy a relationship built on discretion and trust faster than a breach of confidentiality. Even worse, the revealing of a confidential disclosure of sin or weakness in another Christian's life has the potential to destroy that believer, turning him or her away from the church, or even from a walk with the Lord. What Jesus said of those who hurt little children is equally true of those who harm God's children—new, immature Christians:

> *It would be better for him if a millstone were hung around his neck and he were cast into the sea.* (Luke 17:2)

Accountability Requires Confrontation

True accountability involves the confrontation of sin. Therefore, you should be prepared to challenge others and have others challenge your spiritual walk. Nobody looks forward to confronting a brother or sister who is engrossed in sin, but Jesus instructed us to lovingly and delicately confront one another (Matt. 18:15–20). Confrontation is never meant to shame the person caught in sin's clutches, but to help him or her be set free from its power.

The responsibility of confronting another believer about sin is a high and holy one, and it should always humble us. Anybody who is eager or excited about it has the wrong spirit and will likely do more harm than good. The right spirit in confrontation is one of love and deep concern for the erring believer. It is never critical or judgmental, nor does it operate from a feeling of spiritual superiority. It always extends grace and never results in disgrace.

Accountability Requires Confession

One of the most comforting verses in the Bible is 1 John 1:9: "*If we confess our sins, he is faithful and just to forgive us our sins and to cleanse us from all unrighteousness.*" Sin hinders our relationship with a holy God. Therefore, as believers, we need to confess our sins to the Lord.

Many Christians, however, do not have a scriptural understanding of what confession is. They might think it is essentially apologizing to God for wrongs done and thereby being absolved of guilt. Jonathan Dodson clears up much of the ambiguity associated with confession:

> The goal of confession isn't to cleanse ourselves before God, because we can't (Zechariah 3:3-5; Psalm 51:1-2; 1 John 1:7). And it isn't to forgive ourselves because our sin isn't ultimately against self; it's against God (Genesis 39:9; Psalm 51:4). . . . Therefore, confession isn't to be viewed as a ritual bargaining chip we cash in to obtain a clear conscience. Our forgiveness has already been bought in Jesus; we simply procure His purchased forgiveness through confession. . . . Perhaps it would be helpful to think of confession in terms of authenticity. Confession is a verbal way of spiritually recovering our authenticity in Christ.[35]

The Greek word for *confess* literally means to say the same thing about, or to agree with. Biblical confession involves more than merely saying, "I'm sorry. Please forgive me." When we say the same thing God says about our sin, we agree with Him that we must not continue committing it, that we need to make a change in our lives. In reality, biblical confession involves repentance, a change of mind that results in a change of action.

That is where the second level of confession comes in:

Therefore, confess your sins to one another and pray for one another, that you may be healed. The prayer of a righteous person has great power as it is working. (James 5:16)

A believer who is spiritually infected with a recurring sin needs help overcoming it. Even the world recognizes this. Look at Alcoholics Anonymous. The key to its effectiveness is that the alcoholic is a part of a group and is accountable to a sponsor. Its power is in its dynamic: a group of alcoholics helping one another, encouraging each other, being accountable to each other.

This same dynamic defines the D-Group. It is a group of sinners helping each other, praying for each other, encouraging each other, holding each other accountable. This gracious attitude is the heart of Galatians 6:1–3, our marching orders for restoring one another when a sin becomes a stronghold in a believer's life:

Brothers, if anyone is caught in any transgression, you who are spiritual should restore him in a spirit of gentleness. Keep watch on yourself, lest you too be tempted. Bear one another's burdens, and so fulfill the law of Christ. For if anyone thinks he is something, when he is nothing, he deceives himself.

Accountability Requires Compassion

Many, if not most Christians, misunderstand the last statement of Galatians 6:1, mistakenly thinking it means that we must guard ourselves when it comes to restoring another believer who is trapped in sin, lest their sin rub off on us. But nothing could be farther from the spirit of this passage. *The Message,* a paraphrase of the Scripture, captures it well:

If someone falls into sin, forgivingly restore him, saving your critical comments for yourself. You might be needing forgiveness before the day's out. Stoop down and reach out to those who are oppressed. Share their burdens, and so complete Christ's law. If you think you are too good for that, you are badly deceived.

Did you get it? You're a sinner too, and you could be the one needing restoration next. If you don't realize that, Satan has the wool pulled over your eyes. When considering a brother or sister with a sin problem, be careful that you do not say, "I would never do that." When you release those words, you just moved yourself up to the top of some demon's priority list. You might as well say to the devil, "I dare you to try to bring me down." This is why the Bible warns us about this attitude: *"Therefore let anyone who thinks that he stands take heed lest he fall"* (1 Cor. 10:12).

We exemplify Christ's love when we show other sinners the same compassion He showed us. He died that we might be free from sin. We, as His followers, are to live to help one another be victorious over the world, the flesh, and the devil. Compassion has been defined as "your hurt in my heart." Because we are all sinners, compassion should be our response to a brother or sister who is struggling with an area of sin.

Within the D-Group, the leader must assume the responsibility of teaching others about confrontation and confession from Scripture, carefully setting boundaries for how they will operate within the group. The leader must sincerely seek the Lord for discernment in this area, understanding where the others are in their Christian growth, and if they are ready to assume the stewardship of another believer's sins.

Confrontation and confession can only operate within the D-Group when confidentiality and compassion are assured. These are the bases of accountability, and believers who are both humbly transparent and wholeheartedly trustworthy in these areas will develop a bond that is unparalleled in Christian fellowship.

Questions to Consider

What are the four aspects of accountability? Why is each essential?

The Master's Model for Disciple-making

The Bible records that Jesus ministered to three distinct groups: large groups, small groups, and a group of three. Jesus's large group ministry consisted of speaking to crowds, as recorded of the Sermon on the Mount (Matt. 5–7) and of the multitudes who were fed on the hillside. Additionally, a group of 120 believers claimed allegiance to Jesus after his death (Acts 1), and we know of seventy-two who were sent out during His earthly ministry (Luke 10).[36]

Jesus called a group of twelve men to leave their families, friends, and careers to follow him. Subsequently, he invested the remainder of his ministry mentoring this group of twelve disciples. Eugene Peterson, author and pastor, said, "Jesus, it must be remembered, restricted nine-tenths of his ministry to twelve Jews."[37]

Jesus consistently took three disciples with him for intensive times of equipping: Peter, James, and John

(Mark 3:16–17; Luke 6:14). All three were fishermen (Luke 5:10). All three appear together five times in the Gospels:

- At the healing of Peter's mother-in-law (Mark 1:29–31)
- At the raising of Jairus' daughter from the dead (Mark 5:37)
- On the Mount of Transfiguration with Jesus (Mark 9:2)
- At the Olivet Discourse, when Jesus explained end-time events (Mark 13:3)
- With Jesus in the Garden of Gethsemane, just prior to his trial and crucifixion (Matt. 26:37)

The Bible does not present any evidence of Jesus engaging in an ongoing one-on-one discipling relationship with anyone. Jesus definitely met with individuals, such as Nicodemus (John 3) and the woman at the well (John 4), but these were isolated meetings. The Bible also highlights Jesus's intimate relationship with John, and His restoration of Peter on the shore of the Sea of Galilee (John 21). But the Gospels clearly distinguish that Jesus discipled Peter, James, and John as a group.

Please don't hear what I'm *not* saying. I am not suggesting that one-on-one discipling is unscriptural or ineffective. But if you have a choice, I encourage you to meet with three or four others, rather than one. You may be thinking, "What's wrong with a one-on-one mentoring relationship? After all, didn't Jesus pair His disciples?"

Yes, He did, but for an entirely different purpose. Again, notice the wisdom of Solomon: *"Two are better than one . . . And though a man might prevail against one who is alone, two will withstand him—a threefold cord is not quickly broken"* (Eccles. 4:9, 12).

Two are good, but three are better, according to the world's wisest man.

Size Matters

So what is the ideal size of a D-Group? In my experience, four total, as displayed by Jesus, is the number of choice. Any more than five, including you, is too large, and any less than three is too small.[38]

I have also found that the most effective D-Groups are gender-exclusive. Men should meet with men, and women should meet with women. Some topics and personal problems just shouldn't come up in a mixed group. While it is wonderful for couples to study God's Word and grow spiritually together, the crucial dynamic of a D-Group is compromised when couples are involved.

While I have been in a D-Group of two, myself and another person, I discourage this model for five reasons.[39] First, a group of two can be likened to a Ping-Pong match, with you being responsible for keeping the ball in play.

"Mike, how was your day?"

"Good," responds Mike.

The leader probes deeper by asking, "Any insights from your Scripture reading this week?"

"I enjoyed it," Mike briefly replies. The conversation progresses only as the mentor engages the mentee. The pressure to lead is removed when others in the group join in on the spiritual journey collectively.

Second, a one-on-one model is challenging to reproduce because the person in whom you are investing has a tendency to look at you in the same manner that Timothy looked at the apostle Paul. Mentees, after a year or two in a discipling relationship, have said, "I could never do what you did with me with another person." As already mentioned, you are facilitating a group of individuals walking on a journey together. It is worth noting that group members never feel ready to begin their own groups. Neither did the disciples. But Jesus left them with no choice. Remember, the discipling relationship is not complete until the mentee becomes a mentor—the player becomes a coach.

Third, a group of two tends to become a counseling session, where you spend the majority of your time solving personal problems each week. Biblical wisdom for personal issues is certainly a part of the discipling relationship, but therapeutic advice every week must not define the group.

Fourth, as mentioned earlier, Jesus utilized the group model. While He spent time investing in a group of twelve, he used teachable moments to shape three— Peter, James, and John—in a unique way. With the exception of Judas, all of them faithfully followed the Lord, even to the point of death. But these three were the key leaders in the early years of the church.

Solomon was a financial genius, the Warren Buffett of his day. Twenty-five hundred years before Wall Street ever existed, he advocated the diversification of assets (Eccles. 11:1–2). Wise people do not invest all of their funds in one stock for fear of losing their entire life savings, should the company collapse. Instead, good stewards invest in a variety of stocks, bonds, and commodities.

Jesus believed in diversified investing and modeled it in His discipleship example. Joel Rosenberg and T. E. Koshy pose a thought-provoking question: "What if for three years Jesus had discipled only Judas? Despite his best efforts, Jesus would have wound up with no one to carry on his legacy and his message when he returned to the Father. Jesus didn't invest in just one man. He invested in a group of men from a wide range of backgrounds, including fishermen, a tax collector, and a Zealot (a political revolutionary)."[40]

Instead, Jesus poured Himself into twelve men, and, in so doing, taught us the importance of the group in disciple-making. Yes, there are times when a one-on-one mentoring relationship is beneficial; but in the New Testament, particularly the Gospels, it is not the norm.

Paul, in similar fashion, used his missionary journeys to train others. He rarely, if ever, traveled alone, always including Barnabas, Silas, John Mark, Timothy, and others as gospel co-workers. When Paul charged Timothy in his final letter, he stated, *"You then, my child, be strengthened by the grace that is in Christ Jesus, and what you have heard from me in the presence of many witnesses entrust to faithful men who will be able to teach others also"* (2 Tim. 2:1–2). Notice that Paul says, "Entrust to faithful *men* (plural) who will teach others" (emphasis added). Throughout his ministry, Paul modeled this practice.

Finally, a group of three to five provides a built-in accountability system, as well as encouragement from others. In my first D-Group, two of the three men involved attended the first two meetings with their H.E.A.R. journals completed (you will learn about this in chapter 10). One of the guys were skeptical of journaling, and didn't bring a single entry with him that week. Prior to joining the D-Group, his excuse for not reading the Bible was, "It's difficult to understand." Using the other two men to motivate him, I asked, "Can you just try journaling for the next five days? Right now, you have no evidence to prove that it doesn't work. By trying it, you will know if it works for you or not." The next week, he arrived with a smile on his face, saying, "Let me share what I heard from God through His Word this week." Watching the excitement of the others challenged him to contribute to the group, and, therefore, to his own spiritual development.

Questions to Consider

Highlight the benefits of a group of three to five. What are some potential challenges of a group of this size?

The Secret of the Sequoia Trees

In the Muir woods, just north of San Francisco, lies an incredible forest of breath-taking sequoia trees. These trees, reaching almost 250 feet into the sky, are considered to be the largest living things on earth. Many of them have been alive for more than 1,500 years, enduring nature's fiercest winds and storms. What is the secret to their strength? Contrary to what you might think, it is not a deep root system. These trees' roots only descend four feet into the earth, extremely shallow for such immense trees.

The reason for the sequoias' sustained growth is their support system beneath the earth's surface. Sequoia trees only grow in rows or groves. You will never find them growing alone. The roots of these trees interlock with each other, and this is the secret to their survival through the centuries.

What a lesson for the body of Christ! Just as no sequoia grows alone, no believer grows alone.

Memory Verse
John 13:34–35

Chapter 4

NO PAIN, NO GAIN: SPIRITUAL EXERCISE

"Train yourself for godliness; for while bodily training is of some value, godliness is of value in every way, as it holds promise for the present life and also for the life to come."
1 Timothy 4:7–8

"Spiritual disciplines are provided for our good, not for our bondage. They are privileges to be used, not duties to be performed."
Jerry Bridges

We have all seen a late-night infomercial hawking some miraculous workout gadget or gizmo. There is the "Amazing Thighs of Steel," or the latest "Get in Shape Home Workout Station," or the always-popular "Movie Star-Endorsed Exercise Master," right? But keep watching, there's more. "For the first 500 customers that call within the next five minutes, we're going to give you our special DVD, Body of Titanium, and for the next fifty callers, we'll include a free copy of the Elvis Presley Guide to Nutritio—The Later Years."

Whether it's perspiring to old music, the latest doctor-developed contraption, or some Kung Fu video, all of these products make the same promise: follow this plan, and you will get in shape in a matter of days—guaranteed!

The fact is, regardless of which gadget you purchase or which plan you choose, staying healthy requires hard work and commitment. In return for your disciplined efforts, you will live longer, save money on medications, be more productive, sleep better, lose weight, have more energy, and feel healthier, happier, and better about yourself.

In contrast, neglecting exercise has life-affecting and life-threatening consequences. Since clearly everyone has not bought into the value of exercise, let me remind you of a few. You are significantly more vulnerable to a heart attack, heart disease, depression, high blood pressure, weight gain, and diabetes. You are more prone to insomnia, lack of motivation, and lack of productivity. You will lack drive and energy. You will pay more for insurance, if you can get it at all. I'll stop there.

Some of you are surely thinking, "What does this have to do with spiritual growth? I didn't buy this book to be hounded about diet and exercise."

Glad you asked. The Bible says that, in the same manner that we train our bodies, we should discipline our inner man. In fact, Paul, an athlete and sports fan, made a startling statement:

> *Train yourself for godliness; for while bodily training is of some value, godliness is of value in every way, as it holds promise for the present life and also for the life to come.* (1 Tim. 4:7–8)

Did you catch it? Spiritual exercise is more valuable than physical exercise. Like physical exercise, spiritual exercise helps us in *this* life. Like physical exercise, neglecting it has a negative effect on our lives: lack of joy, peace, and happiness; weakness when facing temptation, danger of falling into sin, and lack of self-control; emotional instability and turmoil; worry, doubt, fear, and sleeplessness. . . . I could go on and on.

But physical exercise helps us *only* in this life. Spiritual exercise also helps us in the life to come. Neglecting spiritual exercise has eternal consequences, making it far more valuable. Don't misunderstand what Paul is saying. He is not giving you permission to neglect caring for your body; but he *is* challenging you to be spiritually disciplined.

Point to Ponder

*In your own words,
define godliness.*

Exercising Your Faith

In the same way that we set goals in physical training—to lose weight, lower blood pressure or sugar levels, or have more stamina—spiritual exercise has a goal, and Paul defines it in this passage. What is the goal of spiritual exercise? What is our objective in disciplining ourselves spiritually?

Godliness.

In another letter, Paul explained how God's grace trains us to "renounce ungodliness and worldly passions, and to live self-controlled, upright, and *godly* lives" (Titus 2:11–12). Peter challenged us to practice holiness and *godliness* as we wait for the return of Christ (2 Pet. 3:11–12).

Godliness is neither quickly nor easily attained. Author Jerry Bridges comments on its demands, saying, "This pursuit [of godliness] requires sustained vigorous effort. It allows for no laziness, no half-hearted commitment. In short, it demands the highest priority in a Christian's life."[41]

So what is godliness? You may say, "It is being like God," or, "It is living like Christ," or, "It is producing the fruit of the Spirit." Each of these is correct, but none of them catches its full significance.

In the tedious genealogical records of Noah's ancestors, Scripture highlights only one man, a man whose life defined godliness:

When Enoch had lived 65 years, he fathered Methuselah. Enoch walked with God [there it is] after he fathered Methuselah 300 years and had other sons and daughters. Thus all the days of Enoch were 365 years. Enoch walked with God, and he was not, For God took him. (Gen. 5:21–24)

Enoch's life is eulogized here in eight words: *"He walked with God and he was not."* Talk about a walk to remember. One moment Enoch was walking with God, and the next moment he was caught away into the presence of the Lord.

In the great record of faith heroes, we learn something else about Enoch's godly life:

By faith Enoch was taken up so that he should not see death, and he was not found, because God had taken him. Now before he was taken he was commended as having pleased God. (Heb. 11:5)

Enoch walked with God, and he pleased God. These are the essence of godliness.

Philo, the biblical philosopher and contemporary of Christ, defined godliness as "the right attitude to God and to things divine, the attitude which does not eliminate God altogether, and which does not degenerate into futile superstition, the attitude which gives God the place he ought to occupy in life and in thought and in devotion."[42]

Question to Consider

What can we learn about godliness from the biblical example of Enoch?

The Goal of Godliness

The goal of spiritual exercise is godliness. Through disciplining ourselves spiritually, we shed the excess weight of ungodliness and worldly desires, and build muscle mass of self-control, uprightness, and holiness. Paul is more specific in his letter to the church at Colossae:

> *But now you yourselves are to put off all these: anger, wrath, malice, blasphemy, filthy language out of your mouth. Do not lie to one another, since you have put off the old man with his deeds, and have put on the new man who is renewed in knowledge according to the image of Him who created him. . . . Therefore, as the elect of God, holy and beloved, put on tender mercies, kindness, humility, meekness, longsuffering; bearing with one another, and forgiving one another, if anyone has a complaint against another; even*

as Christ forgave you, so you also must do. But
above all these things put on love, which is the
bond of perfection. (Col. 3:8–14 NKJV)

Notice the terms *put off* and *put on*. There is a vivid image presented here. The Greek words signify taking off and putting on clothes. We come into this world spiritually naked, clothed only in the filth of our inherent sinful nature. As new creations in Christ, we are to take off those filthy qualities (anger, wrath, etc.), and put on the sparkling-clean qualities in which Jesus Christ is clothed (mercies, kindness, humility, etc.).

But we can also paint another picture from these terms. The Greek word for *put off* is the same word used in Hebrews 12:1 for laying aside weight. Greek scholar Kenneth Wuest commented, "The word [weight] is *ogkon* 'bulk, mass,' hence, 'a swelling, superfluous flesh.' The allusion, therefore, is to the training period preparatory to a race in which encumbering superfluity of flesh (fat) is reduced."[43]

Do you see it? Spiritual exercise causes us to lose the fat of our flesh—the old man, our sinful nature—that slows us down in the race of the Christian life, and become lean, mean, godly machines for the glory of Christ. Every believer should strive for godliness.

Plan The Work—Work The Plan

When I was twenty-four, I was hired as a salesman for Powerhouse Gym in Mobile, Alabama. My job was to visit malls, shops, and businesses, and distribute free gym passes to prospects. The goal was that, after trying the facility for a week, they would become members. I quickly noticed something about most of these new members. They half-heartedly went through the motions of exercise for a few weeks and eventually fizzled out. Why? Most people who joined that gym had no real goal of why they were there. They just had an ambiguous notion to get in shape.

So I decided to change my approach to training new members. From that time on, when I signed a person up, I outlined a detailed plan for them, including goals, diet, and schedule. The days of aimless wandering around the gym were over. I would ask, "Mr. Jones, why are you here?"

"Well, I want to get in shape."

"Okay, what does that mean?"

"Well, I want to lose some weight."

"How much weight?"

"Thirty pounds."

"How many days of the week are you going to work out? What times are you going to come to the gym? What is your diet going to look like? How are you structuring your schedule to get a good night's sleep? What supplements are you going to take?"

I observed that those individuals who set goals, drafted a plan of action, and worked that plan were more likely to stay in the gym and achieve their goals than those who had no plan.

Do you remember the saying, "If you aim at nothing, you will hit it every time"? The same is true in your walk with God. One of the reasons people lack the spiritual discipline necessary for growth is because they *fail to begin*—don't miss this—*with the end in mind.*

We must constantly be reminded that our goal is godliness. Donald Whitney said, "Discipline without direction is drudgery."[44] Reading the Bible, praying, fasting, and memorizing Scripture without that goal in mind causes us to lose direction and focus. Without that focus, we will quickly fall into the trap of checking off boxes and merely going through the motions.

However, when we begin with the end in mind, we are continually reminded that the work is worth it, knowing that God is working in us *"both to will and to work for his good pleasure"* (Phil. 2:13).

Do you have spiritual goals for your Christian life? Have you sat down this year and written out your spiritual objectives? What do you want to become for the glory of Christ? You may write down: I desire to be a better husband or father, a better wife or mother. I long for a closer, intimate walk with Christ. I yearn to grow in the faith. I want to share Christ boldly.

Question to Consider

What is the purpose of our pursuit of godliness?

Spiritual Change Agents

God uses three primary change agents to produce godliness in His children: people, circumstances, and spiritual disciplines.[45] We participate passively in the first two, but actively in the third.

People

God uses other people to shape us into the image of Christ. Proverbs 27:17 states, *"As iron sharpens iron, so one man sharpens another"* (NIV). People are divine instruments in God's plan to grow us spiritually. He uses friends, neighbors, co-workers, bosses, and family members. He will use your spouse, your children, your customers, your pastor, music minister, and Sunday school teachers. He even utilizes your enemies and antagonists to bring about change in your life.

Circumstances

In addition to using people, God uses circumstances to help us grow. Romans 8:28 reminds us of this: *"And we know that for those who love God all things work together for good, for those who are called according to His purpose."* God works all things together for good. God uses financial difficulties, physical ailments, trials, tribulation, persecution, setbacks, even the weather—Kandi and I grew closer to the Lord through losing everything we owned in Hurricane Katrina—to mold us into the image of His Son.

Spiritual Disciplines

God also uses spiritual disciplines to develop us. People and circumstances affect us from outside of ourselves, but spiritual disciplines transform us from within. Unlike the first two, you and I have complete control over exercising the spiritual disciplines in our lives. Instead of waiting for God to send some circumstance or individual to help conform us to the image of His Son, we have complete control over the frequency and intensity of our spiritual exercise.

Point to Ponder

List how God has used change agents in your life for spiritual growth.

Spiritual Bonsai Trees

Sadly, many followers of Christ fail to practice spiritual disciplines. Do you remember *The Karate Kid*? Every time Daniel walked into Mr. Miyagi's garage, he found the old man tending to his hobby—trimming bonsai trees.

Most people assume that bonsai trees are naturally dwarfs, but that is not the case. These little trees possess the same DNA as a full-size tree, and they are capable of reaching towering heights. However, due to the tiny pots in which they are raised, bonsai trees grow only twelve to twenty-four inches tall. Their environment restricts their growth.

When you don't take the initiative to practice spiritual disciplines, you become a spiritual bonsai tree. You have the potential—the spiritual DNA of Christ within you—to soar to great heights for the Lord. But you place yourself in a tiny pot when you neglect spiritual exercise, thereby impeding your growth.

Most people have never heard of Angelo Siciliano, but even today, many people remember him by his assumed name, Charles Atlas. Atlas was the guru of bodybuilding in the early- to mid-1900s. The most popular muscleman of his day, Atlas made millions from sales of an exercise program he marketed primarily through comic books. In his ads, a "97-pound weakling" was mocked by his girlfriend after being bullied by a larger, stronger man. The weakling inevitably ordered Atlas' course, followed it, and transformed himself into a manly mass of muscles, like Charles Atlas himself.

The fact is, any man who wants to badly enough can look like Charles Atlas. Most don't want to badly enough, so they do not devote themselves to the disciplined life necessary to achieve that goal. The same is true spiritually when it comes to godliness.

This is why Paul challenges us to *"train [ourselves] for godliness"* (1 Tim. 4:7). Don't be a spiritual weakling! Take matters into your own hands. Discipline yourself and exercise yourself spiritually to achieve godliness.

There are three types of people in this world: those who make things happen, those who watch things happen, and those who wonder what just happened. Be one of those who makes things happen in your spiritual life.

Let's look a little more closely at 1 Timothy 4:7. The New American Standard Bible uses the word *discipline* instead of *train*. The Phillips Translation renders this verse, *"Take the time and the trouble to keep yourself spiritually fit."*[46]

How does this happen? *Discipline* or *train* can be translated as *practice naked*. It is used to describe the training for the Greek games in which the contestants ran without clothes to limit the drag on their bodies during the race. The actual Greek word is *gumnazo*, from which we get our English words "gymnasium" and "gymnastics." In the same way physical exercise affects our bodies, spiritual disciplines train our inner man. When you are disciplined to memorize Scripture, it is like walking on the treadmill. When you spend time in the Word of God, hearing from God in a quiet time, it is like bench-pressing for muscular development.

The "Train" Track

As we dive even deeper into this word, we discover first that it is a singular verb, signifying something that each believer must do individually. You cannot hold others responsible for your spiritual growth. You must take ownership of it yourself.

Second, the verb is in the active tense. Therefore, we assume an active role in our sanctification process. God's Spirit certainly empowers us to grow in holiness, but only through our active, intentional discipline of the sinful nature.

Third, it is an imperative, signifying it is not an option or a multiple-choice scenario; it is a command.

Jesus not only expected His followers to practice these disciplines, He modeled them for us. Did Jesus ever . . .

- pray?
- spend time alone with the Father?
- fast?
- revere and adore the Father?
- share the good news?
- quote the Word of God from memory?

If you read the Gospels, you will find that Jesus did these things all the time. Every Gospel author gives instance after instance of Jesus modeling the spiritual disciplines. If the perfect Son of God practiced spiritual disciplines during His earthly life, how much more do we, as sinful humans, need to incorporate these disciplines into our lives?

Do As I . . .

So if Jesus modeled it, expected it, and challenged us to do it, why don't more believers practice the spiritual disciplines? I think I may know one of the reasons: No one ever took the time to teach them. As you read the Bible, you witness numerous examples of fasting, praying, solitude, worship, and reciting Scripture. The audiences, contemporary to the time, inherently knew how to put these disciplines into practice, even though an instruction manual was never provided for them.

If you were reared in the first century, you were taught these disciplines as a child. They were common knowledge to the hearers in ancient times. From childhood, boys and girls were taught how to pray and memorize Scripture. Everyone knew how to prepare for a fast, follow through without getting weak or dizzy, and end a fast the proper way.

Unfortunately, the same cannot be said for modern believers. Many, if not most, are ill-equipped in the area of spiritual disciplines.

A quick word of caution: just because someone understands all the disciplines and incorporates them, that doesn't guarantee that he or she is growing in the faith. I have met many believers who have grown up in church, read the Bible from cover to cover, and can quote much of the New Testament, but they don't possess a Christ-like attitude. Inward spiritual transformation is more important than routinely going through the motions outwardly. The disciplines are not an end in and of themselves—they are a means to an end . . .

Godliness.

Catch the wind

As you proceed in this book, you are embarking on a journey of spiritual fitness. At times it will seem that you are toiling with all of your strength, but it is actually God at work, forming Christ in you.

We cannot manufacture spiritual change. Only God does that. Nicodemus, a Pharisee and member of the Sanhedrin, sought wisdom from Jesus one night. Jesus responded, *"The wind blows where it wishes, and you hear its sound, but you do not know where it comes from or where it goes. So it is with everyone who is born of the Spirit"* (John 3:8).

What does that mean? Jesus is saying that the wind blows wherever it wants to. We don't know where it comes from, and we don't know where it goes. We only see its effects. In the same manner, the Holy Spirit works in us in order that Christ can work through us (Col. 1:29; Phi. 2:12–13).

Pastor and author John Ortberg explains how this looks in our lives:

> It's the difference between piloting a motorboat or a sailboat. We can run a motorboat all by ourselves. We can fill the tank and start the engine. We are in control. But a sailboat is a different story. We can hoist the sails and steer the rudder, but we are utterly dependent on the wind. The wind does the work. If the wind doesn't blow and sometimes it doesn't, we sit still in the water no matter how frantic we act. Our task is to do whatever enables us to catch the wind.[47]

Will you hoist your sails over the next few weeks and catch the Wind? Will you put on your spiritual running shoes and join me in disciplining our inner selves for godliness?

Questions to Consider

What steps can you take to discipline your inner man? What course corrections need to be made in your life today?

Memory Verse
1 Timothy 4:7–8

Chapter 5

C.L.O.S.E.R.

COMMUNICATE: KNOCKING ON HEAVEN'S DOOR

"Ask, and it will be given to you; seek, and you will find; knock, and it will be opened to you."
Matthew 7:7

"You can do more than pray after you have prayed; but you can never do more than pray until you have prayed."
A. J. Gordon

From the beginning of my journey as a believer, I have understood the importance of prayer. But it wasn't until I pastored my first church that I developed a passion for it.

Jody visited our church one Sunday morning. After the service, he asked if I would be interested in praying with him. He invited me to meet him the next morning at 7:30 in the McDonald's parking lot. I assumed we would drink a cup of coffee, eat an Egg McMuffin, and talk for a while. But I was wrong. When I spotted him in the parking lot, he motioned me over to his car. Jody then called Doug, his prayer partner, and the three of us entered into a time of prayer.

We never made it inside the restaurant that day, praying instead in the parking lot for almost an hour. After finishing his prayer, Jody concluded by saying, "Okay, brother, I will see you next week—same time, same place." I walked back to my truck saying to myself, "What about the coffee and Egg McMuffin?"

For the next four months, we prayed together every Monday morning in the McDonald's parking lot. Later, because of changes in our schedules, we prayed by phone rather than in person.

During this time, we simply couldn't get enough of praying with other people. We found ourselves calling friends and family to ask, "How can we pray for you today?" After exchanging requests, we would then offer our petitions and supplications to the Lord.

Over time, our manner of praying changed. Instead of merely asking God to address our checklist of requests, we focused on praying for things that we discerned truly mattered to Him. I had learned a revolutionary truth about prayer: as I prayed, I was changed. My desires changed. My priorities changed. My way of thinking changed. The things that once mattered most to me were no longer at the top of the list. God had revealed more of Himself to me as I prayed, and, as a result, I was changed.

When was the last time you asked the Lord to reveal to you the things that matter most to Him? We are quick to ask for what we desire or feel that we need, but rarely do we ask for what God desires. We are prone to pray according to our perspective, seldom seeking to see through God's eyes. Perhaps the greatest benefit of a life committed to prayer is that, as we pray, God's Spirit communicates with our spirit, and He changes us from within.

Question to Consider

On a scale of one to ten, with ten being the highest, how would you rate your prayer life?

Seminar on Prayer

Throughout His earthly ministry, Jesus taught His disciples many things, but Luke 11 captures the first and only time in Scripture when the disciples asked Jesus for instruction on a specific activity. The Bible says,

> *Now Jesus was praying in a certain place, and when he finished, one of his disciples said to him, "Lord, teach us to pray, as John taught his disciples." (Luke 11:1)*

Notice what these guys *didn't* inquire about. Systematic theology. Church growth and leadership. Healing, preaching, or walking on water.

The disciples had learned that prayer was the source of all things. Of all the courses they could have selected to be taught by Jesus Himself, they chose the discipline of prayer. Through observing Jesus's prayer life—His commitment to spending time with His Father and the way He spoke to God—they wanted to pray like He did. Since Jesus demonstrated power in His prayer life, His closest followers desired to learn from Him. His example caused them to thirst for something more in their own lives and ministries. And because they asked, Jesus used the opportunity not only to instruct them, but us as well.

85

Pray the Way Jesus Explained It

Imagine how you would have felt at this moment. The disciples were about to listen to the greatest prayer warrior of all teach on the subject of prayer. All were silent, and Jesus held their undivided attention. Picture the twelve sitting around the Lord with their sharpened pencils and opened notebooks. They were ready for a lengthy lecture on prayer, but before they could even get comfortable in their seats, it was over, and Jesus moved on to His next point. Surely both their pencils and their mouths dropped as they thought, "What?"

In just forty English words, Jesus had explained how to pray. What Jesus didn't say still speaks louder today than what He actually did say. Our Lord's brevity teaches the most vital prayer lesson of all:

Prayer is not learned in a classroom.

The most crucial words in this crash course are the first three: *"When you pray . . ."* We do not learn how to pray by going to prayer conferences. We do not learn how to pray by reading books on the subject. There is only one way to cultivate an intimate, effective prayer life:

Pray, pray, pray.

Even though you may study a foreign language, the only way to truly learn it is to speak it. Prayer is similar; you learn it by doing it. Prayer is learned experientially. Jesus, through His silence, is saying, "Listen, prayer is not about filling your mind with knowledge on ways to pray. Prayer is about *doing* it, so start praying."

Andrew Murray, speaking of the practice of prayer in his book *With Christ in the School of Prayer*, commented, "Reading a book about prayer, listening to lectures and talking about it is good, but it won't teach you to pray. You get nothing without exercise, without practice. I might listen for a year to a professor of music playing the most beautiful music, but that won't teach me to play an instrument."[48] A powerful prayer life is developed through the practice of actually praying.

Questions to Consider

Consider the disciples' request, "Lord, teach us to pray" in Luke 11:1. What prompted them to make this request? What are some ways you can improve your prayer life?

Father and Friend

Many believers never experience an effective, fulfilling prayer life because they never truly understand the nature of prayer. With two words—father and friend—Jesus taught us that prayer is personal, relational, and intimate. He begins and ends this passage with the word *Father*:

". . . Father, hallowed be your name . . ." (Luke 11:2)

". . . how much more will the heavenly Father give the Holy Spirit to those who ask him." (Luke 11:13)

In Matthew's account of the Lord's Prayer, Jesus begins with, *"Our Father"* (Matt. 6:9), reminding us that we have a personal relationship with God. When we receive Christ, we are adopted as sons and daughters of God. The Father places us into His family. Because we are His children, we can freely call upon Him.

Paul taught us not only to address God personally, but also affectionately as *"Abba, Father"* (Rom. 8:15; Gal. 4:6). *Abba* is like the endearing names we commonly use, such as *daddy* or *papa*. Mark records that in the Garden of Gethsemane—in His darkest hours—our Savior addressed God in this intensely personal way. One way to radically change your prayer life is to start referring to God as "Daddy."

Immediately after He gave the Lord's Prayer, Jesus taught another lesson about our relationship with God. In order that we might fully grasp this truth, He shared a parable about three friends:

> *Which of you who has a friend will go to him at midnight and say to him, "Friend, lend me three loaves, for a friend of mine has arrived on a journey, and I have nothing to set before him."*
> (Luke 11:5–6)

God is our Friend! Notice how the man in this parable didn't hesitate to awaken his friend at midnight because he needed his help. In the same way, we should never hesitate to call upon God. He is our true Friend, always ready to help us. Never think twice about calling on Him. We cannot inconvenience Him. He has everything we need, and He wants to share it with us.

A Pattern to Follow

Most of us, at some time in our lives, have recited the Lord's Prayer. In many churches, it is a regular part of worship. There is nothing wrong with quoting the Lord's Prayer, as long as it is not merely a meaningless ritual. However, Jesus's original intention for it was different. What we call the Lord's Prayer is actually an outline for us to pray by. Think of it as a skeleton. As we pray, we are to put flesh and skin on these bones:

> *Our Father in heaven, hallowed be Your name. Your kingdom come, Your will be done, on earth as it is in heaven. Give us this day our daily bread, and forgive us our debts, as we also have forgiven our debtors. And lead us not into temptation, but deliver us from evil. [Thine is the kingdom and the power and the glory forever. Amen]* (Matt. 6:9–13)

In this outline, Jesus gave us six components for our prayers:

- *Praise:* **Our Father, who art in heaven**
- *Purpose:* **Your will be done, on earth as it is in heaven**
- *Provision:* **Give us our daily bread**
- *Pardon:* **Forgive us our debts (trespasses, sins)**
- *Protection:* **Lead us not into temptation, but deliver us from evil**
- *Praise* (again): **Thine is the kingdom and the power and the glory.**

Notice that offering praise to God both begins and ends the prayer.

Jesus intended for His model prayer to be used as a springboard for us into the refreshing, life-sustaining waters of intimate, effective prayer. Here is an example of how to pray using this model:

- *Praise:* "Father, heaven is Your throne and the earth is Your footstool. You have formed me with Your own hands. You knew me in my mother's womb. You and You alone are worthy to be worshipped."

89

- *Purpose:* "All things work together for good according to Your purpose. Because You pre-destined me to be conformed to the image of Your own Son before the world was formed, I am not my own. You bought me with a price. Guide me, direct me, and correct me in Your ways. Help me say, 'Not my will, Lord, but Your will be done.'"

- *Provision:* "I will not worry about the things that I need, for just like the birds of the air are cared for, You provide for me. You're my Shepherd; therefore I shall not want any-thing. Everything I need, You supply. Great is Your faithfulness to me. You know my finan-cial situation better than my own accountant, so why should I worry?"

- *Pardon:* "When I confess my sins to You, Lord, You are faithful and just to forgive me. You wash them away as far as the east is from the west. Forgive me for my sins against you. If I have wronged others, reveal that to me so that I can make things right with them."

- *Protection:* "I have nothing to fear, Lord, because You are with me. Your right hand upholds me. Whether I am in the lowest valley or on the high-est mountain, You never forsake me, and You never leave me. Thank You, God, for never leav-ing me. You're always with me. You're my Rock and my Redeemer. I can do all things through You because You strengthen me. If You are for me, God, who can be against me?"

- *Praise:* "You are worthy to be praised and wor-shipped. Blessed be Your holy name. AMEN."

Following the pattern Jesus gave us, add the details of your life. What has God done for you that you can praise Him for? What do you need? What temptations are you facing? What are your sins? Whom are you struggling to forgive?

Make it personal. Make it specific. Make it real.

Walking Point

Rewrite the disciples' prayer in your own words (Matt. 6:9–13). Make it personal, highlighting relevant issues in your life.

How Big is Your Rock Pile?

God knows that we are forgetful, so He created a system to reduce our lapses of memory. Standing at the banks of the Jordan, the people of Israel were eager to enter the Promised Land. One obstacle stood in their way—deep, rushing water. Instantly, when the priests' feet touched the water, the stream backed up. It was as if someone had turned off a faucet somewhere upstream. Consequently, the nation of Israel (somewhere between a half-million to two million people) followed the priests across the dry river bed. As soon as they crossed, water resumed flowing. God kept his promise to lead them into the Promised Land, and He did so in a miraculous manner.

After crossing the Jordan, the Israelites were instructed to appoint twelve men, each representing one of the twelve tribes of Israel, to build a rock pile. The reason?

That this may be a sign among you. When your children ask in time to come, "What do those

*stones mean to you?" then you shall tell them that
the waters of the Jordan were cut off before the
ark of the covenant of the LORD. When it passed
over the Jordan, the waters of the Jordan were
cut off. So these stones shall be to the people of
Israel a memorial forever.* (Josh. 4:6–7)

In a day without journals, computers, or electronic
reminders, God used a pile of rocks to imprint His supernatural intervention upon their minds. "Don't ever
forget what I did for you," the Lord said. "Generation
after generation will remember My faithfulness."

Throughout Joshua, God continued to work supernaturally, prompting the people to erect stone memorials seven times.[49] Many people pray for God to work in
their lives, but how many actually keep a record of His
faithfulness? These spiritual stones—records of God's
faithfulness—will fortify your faith during the difficult
seasons of life. Again and again, they will be platforms
for praise. Forgetting God's goodness is not an option
in His kingdom.

One way to remember God's goodness is by keeping
a prayer journal (see Appendix 5 for an example). Just
as the Israelites erected stones marking the movement
of the Lord (Josh. 4), your prayer log is a way of marking God's faithfulness for the future. It will continually prompt you to praise the Lord for His goodness
and steadfast love. Whatever your request is, whether
it is for a family member to enter into a relationship
with Jesus, or for personal guidance from God, write
it down.

In addition to recording your requests in a journal,
record the date you first made the request and the date
God answered it. This practice is essential because it
gives you the opportunity to rejoice over answered
prayers, as well as to provide a testimony to others of

God's goodness. Sharing your journal will encourage others to pray as well.

While you can use your prayer journal in a group setting, the benefits will blossom during private prayer and reflection. Additionally, what better legacy can you leave to your children and grandchildren than a written record of your prayers—including those prayed for them—and God's faithfulness in answering?

Questions to Consider

What spiritual stones need to be stacked in your life? How big is your rock pile?

Pray Persistently

In addition to Jesus's six components for prayer, Scripture also gives us six commands as to how we should pray. The first is found at the end of Jesus's parable about the three friends:

And I tell you, ask, and it will be given to you; seek, and you will find; knock, and it will be opened to you. (Luke 11:9)

Literally translated, the Greek verb tense used in this verse is, "keep on asking, keep on seeking, and keep on knocking." Simply stated, Jesus commanded us to be persistent in our prayers. Sadly, few Christians pray this way. Most pray randomly or irregularly. When you are tempted to be lazy and undisciplined in prayer, or when you are becoming discouraged because your prayer hasn't been answered, remember the promise of Jesus: if you keep asking, you will receive; if you keep seeking, you will find; and if you keep knocking, it will be opened for you. In your own life, are you guilty of giving up on God?

Do you know what the word *persistence* means? It means to hold on, to press on, to keep on keeping on until God answers or the door is opened. It is not some meaningless performance; it is a restless passion in your heart. It is an all-consuming fire, an inner compulsion that drives you to tenaciously cry out to God to work, remembering all the while that He sovereignly works all things together for good.

Scotland was reformed because John Knox persistently prayed, "Lord, give me Scotland or I'll die!"[50] Believers should pray with this kind of steely resolve. The "Prince of Preachers," Charles Spurgeon, explained,

> God will bless Elijah and send rain on Israel, but Elijah must pray for it. If the chosen nation is to prosper, Samuel must plead for it. If the Jews are to be delivered, Daniel must intercede. God will bless Paul, and the nations shall be converted through him, but Paul must pray. Pray he did without ceasing; his epistles show that he expected nothing except by asking for it. If you may have everything by asking, and nothing without asking, I beg you to see how absolutely vital prayer is, and I beseech you to abound in it.[51]

Pray Privately

> *"But when you pray, go into your room and shut the door and pray to your Father who is in secret. And your Father who sees in secret will reward you."* (Matt. 6:6)

In this crowded, noisy, and busy world, the only way to make sure you are praying privately is to carve out time to get alone with the Lord. If you fail to plan, then you can plan to fail. Plan time into your schedule to pray. We prioritize our lives around what is important. Is time alone with the Lord a priority to you? How often do you depart from the hustle and bustle of life to be refreshed by the Lord?

Poor praying is a result of poor planning. One system to consider is what we might call "7 Up." Here is how it works: pray every morning for the next seven days for seven minutes, as soon as you wake up. In order to track your progress, note the time that you begin praying.

Hopefully, you are thinking, "I can do that." Because you can. But seven minutes of prayer is longer than you think! Most of those who have accepted this challenge initially respond by saying, "I prayed for myself, my friends, my family, and everyone else that came to mind. I was sure that I prayed for at least ten minutes; but after looking at the clock, only four minutes had passed." If you have never spent seven continuous minutes in prayer, expect it to be challenging at first. Don't give up. Press on, and soon seven minutes will turn into ten, then twenty, then even more.

Questions to Consider

What changes must you make in your schedule in order to rise early for prayer?

Pray Publicly

The biblical model of prayer always included participatory, public prayer. Sometimes we call this "corporate prayer." Think of how often the apostles and the early church met together to pray (Acts 2:42; 4:23–31).

You might be thinking, "In my busy, fully-scheduled, fast-paced world, how can I find time to come to the church and pray?" Years ago, people could easily walk over to the local church or a neighbor's house to pray together. Today's culture of traveling miles and miles through traffic to attend church can make this a tough task to accomplish.

But that is not an excuse. Like everything else, a robust prayer life is a matter of priorities and commitment. If it is important enough to you, and if you are committed to it, then you will do it. The same people who say it is too difficult to drive to a prayer meeting think nothing at all of driving to the gym, or the tanning bed, or the coffeehouse every day!

When praying with a prayer partner or several people, ask for requests, and then take turns praying for one another. Because of our busy schedules, it may be impossible to meet at church for a prayer meeting during the day. But with our modern technology, we don't have to be in the same room to pray together. We have a thousand options for how we can stay connected anywhere and anytime. How about a Facebook prayer meeting? Or Zoom? Or just a simple phone call?

What if you connected with two different people every day for prayer? In one week, you could pray with fourteen people. You may be saying, "I don't have the time to pray like that every day." What if you had prayer on the phone only once a week? You would still have prayed with two more people than you would have otherwise.

Pray Precisely

> *"What father among you, if his son asks for a fish, will instead of a fish give him a serpent; or if he asks for an egg, will give him a scorpion? If you then, who are evil, know how to give good gifts to your children, how much more will the heavenly Father give the Holy Spirit to those who ask him!"* (Luke 11:11–13)

The primary principle in this passage is that God is a loving Father who delights in giving His children what they desire. But there is a second principle here that is often overlooked: the son in Jesus's illustration asked for something specific, and his father gave him specifically what he asked for. He asked for a fish, and his father gave him a fish. He asked for an egg, and an egg is what he received.

Previously, in this same message, Jesus again modeled this principle of praying specifically. The man who went to his neighbor at midnight did not ask, "Can I borrow something to eat?" He didn't even say, "Lend me some bread." He specifically requested, "Friend, lend me three loaves" (Luke 11:5).

James wrote, *"You do not have, because you do not ask"* (James 4:2). Many people pray, but they never really ask God for anything. They pray only in general terms:

- "Lord, please help everybody to get saved."
- "Please bless all of the missionaries."
- "Heal the sick people."
- "Forgive all of my sins."
- "Meet all of my needs."

When you pray, pray for specific people to be saved—by name. Pray for specific missionaries, those you know or whom your church supports. Pray for sick people you know, or who are on your prayer list at church, or who are connected to people you know. Confess your sins specifically. Tell God exactly what you need.

How can you otherwise track God's answers to your prayers? Unspecific prayers are powerless prayers, and they are an insult to a God who genuinely loves people, One who invites us to join Him in His great work through prayer.

Pray Confidently, in Faith

One way to make sure your prayer life is powerless is to pray with low expectations. Have you ever been guilty of praying, and, at the same time, doubting if God can or will answer? James warned us about this:

> *But let him ask in faith, with no doubting, for the one who doubts is like a wave of the sea that is driven and tossed by the wind. For that person must not suppose that he will receive anything from the Lord; he is a double-minded man, unstable in all his ways.* (James 1:6–8)

After coming down from the Mount of Transfiguration, Jesus was approached by a man whose son was possessed by a demon. The disciples were unable to heal the boy, so the father approached Jesus for help saying,

> *Lord, have mercy on my son, for he is an epileptic and he suffers terribly. For often he falls into the fire, and often into the water. And I brought him to your disciples, and they could not heal him.* (Matt. 17:15–16)

Jesus was indignant because His disciples had access to the power of God but were unable to heal the man's son. After being questioned by Jesus, the father responded, *"I believe, help my unbelief!"* (Mark 9:24). Later that day, the disciples asked Jesus to explain the reason for their failure. Pointing out their *little faith,* Jesus rebuked them for their unbelief. They were powerless because they were faithless.

Do you expect God to move when you pray, or do you simply go through the motions of praying? Scripture is clear that God acts according to His will and purpose (Rom. 8:28), but at the same time, He commands us to seek Him in prayer (Luke 11:9; Matt. 7:7). Remember the words of James, *"You do not have, because you do not ask"* (James 4:2). Also, keep in mind that prayer is not just about what we receive from God. Prayer changes us. Often in my own prayer life, my requests have been altered after spending long periods with God.

Start asking and expecting God to move. Pray in faith, fully confident that God will answer according to His will and in His time.

Question to Consider

Have you ceased praying for something or someone because God hasn't answered on your timetable?

Pray Constantly, Throughout the Day

While getting alone with the Lord is important and should be a part of our daily lives, it is not the only time or way that we should pray. One of the shortest verses in the Bible teaches the true essence of prayer:

"Pray without ceasing." (1 Thess. 5:17)

Many read this simple command and ask, "How is that possible? I can't just drop everything and pray all of the time." Through the centuries, some have taken this verse to the extreme and adopted a monastic lifestyle: they have removed themselves from society, shut themselves away from the rest of the world, and done nothing but pray.

That is not what this verse is suggesting, and it is not the example of Jesus or any New Testament believers. In fact, it is exactly the opposite of what Jesus and the apostles modeled.

So what does this verse mean? How do we pray without ceasing?

As discussed earlier, it is important to have a formal, dedicated time of prayer each day. It is good to begin a prayer with the words, "Our Father," and to end it with, "In Jesus's name, amen." But it is not a rule that we must do that all of the time.

To pray without ceasing is to begin your day with "Our Father"—to establish a connection with God, and then keep it open throughout the day. When you need direction, ask Him for it. When you need wisdom, ask Him for it. When you are tempted, call upon Him to deliver you. When somebody provokes you and you are struggling to keep your mouth shut, call upon Him for self-control. When somebody blesses you, thank Him for it.

Begin each day with "Our Father" and end it with "In Jesus's name, amen." In between, talk to God all day long. Include Him in everything that happens in your life. Call on Him for wisdom, strength, direction, deliverance, and anything else you need. Lift up others' needs to Him as His Spirit brings them to your mind. Thank Him immediately for every blessing and good thing in your day. Praise Him and tell Him you love Him. Share every joy and every sorrow with Him. This is what it means to pray without ceasing.

Who Needs it the Most?

The Lord's Prayer starts with the character and person of God. Likewise, many of the Psalms begin by declaring God's holiness, righteousness, sovereignty, and love. After focusing your attention on God, pray for the person who needs it most—you. Before you can help others, you yourself must be at peace with God.

Next, pray for those closest to you, such as your spouse, your children, and your family. Then, pray for your church family, friends, and coworkers (see Appendix 11 for a prayer guide).

Get into the habit of praying Scripture. Praying Scripture includes praying actual prayers that are in the Bible, and also communicating back to God the scriptural statements about His character, His promises, and His love. The book of Acts and the Epistles contain many prayers by the apostle Paul that can be applied to your life (Eph. 1:15–23; 3:14–21; Col. 1:11–14).

A simple formula followed by many in their prayer life is known by the acrostic, *A.C.T.S.:* Adoration, Confession, Thanksgiving, and Supplication. This format may be helpful. The most important thing to remember is that prayer is a natural, comfortable conversation between you and your Father, between you and a Friend. Don't worry about how to do it. Just do it!

Walking Point

List three people who are far from God for whom you can pray over the next few weeks. Follow up by taking them to lunch to talk about their spiritual condition.

Weapons of Mass Distraction

Recently, I became heavily convicted about how much time I spend in prayer. Allow me to be completely transparent for a moment. I am a pastor. I pray every day. I pray in the morning. I pray with my two boys before they go to bed every night. I have a prayer partner with whom I pray daily. I pray with others on numerous occasions. Assessing all of this made me feel good about my prayer life . . .

Until I compared how much time I actually pray to how much time I spend engaged in things that just don't matter.

Watching TV, surfing the web, observing people on Facebook, playing video games—you can substitute whatever distracts you—is equivalent to mental thumb-twiddling.

Think about this for a minute: Have you ever lost anything by missing the final episode of a reality show? Has your life been enriched by binge watching a new TV series or marathoning *The Office* again?

These things may not be bad by themselves, but distractions come in all kinds of innocuous forms. The excitement associated with winning fades as soon as the season is over. Can anyone tell me who won the World Series in 1984? Some of you can, which is fine, but in the realm of eternity, how does it matter?

Think of the hours you waste watching online videos, reading tweets, perusing Facebook posts, surfing the Internet, posting pictures, monitoring items on eBay, pinning recipes, or playing games on your gaming system. I am not implying that these things are wrong in and of themselves, but think of the *hours* you *waste* on them.

The Bible commands us to make the best use of our time (Eph. 5:16). I wonder if, at the Judgment Seat of Christ, Jesus will have a record of how much time we wasted on these kinds of things. Somehow, I suspect that He will, and we will have to answer for it.

Participate in an exercise for a minute. Draw a vertical line in your mind. On the left, assess the time you spend in prayer and the Word on any given week. On the right, estimate how much time you spend on TV, technology, and other forms of entertainment or recreation.

Is conviction setting in for you yet? It did for me.

We wonder why we aren't growing in our relationship with Christ. We wonder why we aren't seeing more of God in our lives. We wonder why our churches aren't filled with the presence and power of God.

Do something about it. Conviction without action is worthless. Poor praying comes from poor planning. First, identify the distractions in your life. Next, ruthlessly eliminate them. Replace the free time in your life with prayer and studying the Word.

For forty days leading up to Palm Sunday and Easter, many Christians reflect on the suffering of Christ by observing Lent, a period of fasting, repentance, and spiritual discipline. This year, I decided to turn the TV off—for forty days. No sports, no movies, no shows, no news.

I can honestly say that I have never felt closer to the Lord than during those forty days. I can give you testimony after testimony of God's goodness and grace during that time. It wasn't that God wasn't with me prior to my forty-day period of abstaining from television. He was.

The problem was, I couldn't hear Him clearly. The distractions had numbed my mind and desensitized my soul to His voice.

Walking Points

*Consider abstaining from the gadget
or activity you enjoy most for a
season. Replace that time you spend
with the Word and prayer.*

Memory Verse
Philippians 4:6–7

 *Chapter 6*

C.L.O.S.E.R.
LEARN: MINING FOR GOLD

"Study to show thyself approved, rightly
dividing the word of truth."
2 Timothy 2:15

"Ignorance of Scripture is ignorance of Christ."
Jerome

"I can't understand the Bible!"

This often-used excuse by people who don't read God's Word is one of the most untrue lies you can believe about yourself.

As a Christian, your relationship with God and your relationship with the Bible are inseparable. God has revealed Himself to us in His Word. We cannot know God apart from the Bible. God has revealed everything we need to know for the Christian life in the pages of His Holy Word. It is through the truth of God's Word that we *"grow up in every way into him"* (Eph. 4:15). Scripture completely equips us, making us competent for every good work God has created us to do (2 Tim. 3:17). You cannot be a true disciple of Christ apart from His Word. You cannot grow as a Christian without the Bible.

Do not fall for Satan's lie that you cannot understand the Bible. Why would God go to supernatural lengths to give us His Word, and then make it difficult for us to understand?

Still, many sincere believers feel intimidated when they open their Bibles. Every Christian, at some point in his or her life, has asked, "How can I understand the Bible?" or, "How can I know what the Bible really means?" or, "How do I study the Bible?" In this chapter, we are going to answer these questions by showing you how to study the Bible and arrive at the intended meaning of a verse or passage.

God Said What He Meant

Two dangerous extremes exist in churches when it comes to understanding the meaning of Scripture. Through the centuries, some have taught that ordinary people like you and me cannot understand the Bible, saying that only Christ's special representative on earth, who is the head of their church, can interpret Scripture. They conclude that we should not attempt to read it on our own.

At the other end of the spectrum are those who teach that the Bible has no definite meaning. It is completely subjective: whatever you think the Bible means, whatever you think it is saying to you at the time, is what it means.

Here's the simple truth: God said what He meant in Scripture, and He meant what He said. Every word of every verse of every chapter of every book has a meaning given by God when He breathed it out through the human writers. Grasp what God says about Scripture:

Knowing this first of all, that no prophecy of Scripture comes from someone's own interpretation. For no prophecy was ever produced by the will of man, but men spoke from God as they were carried along by the Holy Spirit. (2 Pet. 1:20–21)

The truth is, we can understand what God means in any passage of the Bible. While Christ has given the church pastors and teachers to help us understand His Word (Eph. 4:11–15), the Lord gave each of us an even greater Gift: the Holy Spirit. He is our Helper in understanding the Bible:

Now we have received not the spirit of the world, but the Spirit who is from God, that we might understand the things freely given us by God. And we impart this in words not taught by human wisdom but taught by the Spirit, interpreting spiritual truths to those who are spiritual. The natural person does not accept the things of the Spirit of God, for they are folly to him, and he is not able to understand them because they are spiritually discerned. (1 Cor. 2:12–14)

Every genuine believer receives a wonderful Gift at the time of salvation: the Holy Spirit literally comes into us and dwells within our bodies. Jesus taught us that one of the invaluable things the Spirit does for us is guide us into all truth. He takes the things of Christ and reveals them to us (John 16:13–14). With His help, we can—without human intervention—understand the Bible for ourselves.

Our task then, when we open our Bibles, is to arrive at the meaning God intended for the passage we are reading. In theological circles, this process is called *hermeneutics*, a big word which simply means to explain or interpret. Taken directly from a Greek word, its verb form is used in Jesus's teaching on the road to Emmaus:

> *And beginning with Moses and all the Prophets, he **interpreted** to them in all the Scriptures the things concerning himself.* (Luke 24:27)

Other versions translate this word as "expounded" (KJV, NKJV) and "explained" (NASB, NIV, NLT).

There are many principles involved in hermeneutics, and many excellent books have been written which teach these principles. As you grow as a Christian, you may want to dig in to some of these books to help you sharpen your skills (see Appendix 10 for a list of resources). But you do not have to master all of these to understand the Bible for yourself. A few primary skills will enable you to discern—with the Holy Spirit's help—what God means in His Word, and how it applies to your life.

The Inductive Bible Study Method has been a standard approach to understanding God's Word for many years. Bible teacher Kay Arthur popularized this threefold process of observation, explanation, and application in her book *How to Study the Bible*.[52] When we follow this approach, our understanding of the text will be formed by the facts of the Word, not by our own opinions or ideas about the text. Our goal when studying the Bible is to draw the meaning *out of* the text, and not to force our own understanding *into* it.

Remember, while any passage of Scripture can be applied to our lives in many ways, every passage has only *one* meaning intended by God when He gave it through the human writer. Memorize this simple rule: *One interpretation, many applications.*

Questions to Consider

*Have you ever had a difficult time
understanding God's Word?
If so, has it made you want
to quit reading it?*

Priority #1: *Context*

Many people buy in to the idea that the reader's perception of a biblical text determines its meaning. Nothing can carry you farther from the truth of God's Word than this fallacy. The cardinal rule of biblical interpretation is *the meaning of the text is established by what the original author intended.* The writer, under the inspiration of the Holy Spirit (2 Pet. 1:21), established the meaning of the passage the day he wrote it. Our role as students of the Bible is to uncover what the original author intended to communicate to his original audience. A text cannot mean something today that it did not mean when it was originally written.

The primary key to understanding the writer's intended meaning of a text is identifying its context. Simply defined, the context of a statement, verse, or passage is the setting in which it is spoken or written. "When it comes to interpreting and applying the Bible, context is crucial. In fact, we would go so far as to say that the most important principle of biblical interpretation is that context determines meaning.[53]

The context of a passage includes the verses before and after it. The more surrounding verses you read, the better you will grasp the context of a verse or passage. For example, in order to understand John 3:16, it would be helpful to read John 3:15 and John 3:17. But if you really want to grasp John 3:16, you should read the entire third chapter of John. However, the context extends beyond the immediate chapter. By understanding the perspective from which John presents the life of Christ in his Gospel, you have an even clearer understanding of John 3:16.

You should also consider the person to whom Jesus originally spoke this verse. Nicodemus was a Pharisee, a man who lived and breathed by the teachings of the law. In John 3:16, Jesus emphasized to this legalist that salvation is not by works, but by faith. By backing up to verses 14 and 15, you see that Jesus was pointing Nicodemus to His approaching death on the cross. Therefore, saving faith is faith in the substitutionary death of Christ as the atonement for sin.

Do you see the point? Scripture, starting with the Old Testament and continuing throughout the New, is a tapestry woven together with a continuous, logical flow of thoughts, words, paragraphs, chapters, and sections. This is why context helps out the meaning of a text. Every verse of the Bible is connected to the verses around it, the book in which it appears, the Testament in which it is set, and the message of the entire Bible.

Identifying the context is like using the zoom feature of a camera. The more you zoom out, the more you are able to see. To fully understand the meaning of a verse or passage, you have to zoom out enough to see the complete picture.

Zoologists know that, to truly understand an animal, it must be studied in its natural habitat. Do you remember dissecting frogs in biology class? Opening up the frog and picking it apart reveals what makes its body function. However, dissecting it reveals nothing about the way it lives—its birth patterns, breeding practices, the tone of its croak. In order to appreciate the frog, we must put it back in its habitat, on the lily pad where it resided. Only in its environment are we able to clearly gain insight into its life. In the same manner, a biblical text can only be understood when it is examined within the setting in which it was written—its habitat or environment, its context.

By studying a passage of the Bible in its correct context, you will discover what the original author intended to communicate to his original audience. When we fail to identify the context of a passage, we will likely misunderstand it. A verse or statement plucked out of its original context can be misconstrued to prove anything. The classic example of this is Psalm 14:1, which states, "There is no God." But look at the entire verse:

The fool says in his heart, "There is no God."
They are corrupt, they do abominable deeds, the
is none who does good.

The context makes all the difference.

Questions to Consider

Why is context important to interpretation?
What happens if the context of the passage
is not taken into consideration?

Observation—What Does the Text Say?

The first step in the Inductive Bible Study Method is *observation*. In order to familiarize yourself with the text, begin by reading, rereading, and reading again the passage at hand. G. Campbell Morgan, who pastored the Westminster Chapel in London, is one of my favorite preachers of days gone by. Morgan would read a book of the Bible *fifty times* before he even lifted his pen to prepare a sermon. "How many times should *I* read the text?" you may ask. The answer is, as many times as it takes for it to begin to take root in your heart.

After familiarizing yourself with the text, engage it by asking the six basic investigative questions about the passage: *who, what, when, where, why,* and *how.* Here are some examples of how to use investigative questions to make observations:

Who is the author?

Who are the recipients?

Who are the main characters involved in the text?

What is happening in the text?

What is the author intending to communicate?

What are key words in the text?

What is the context of this verse?

What important comparisons or contrasts do you see?

When do the events take place?

Where do these events take place?

Why do the events take place?

Why was this text written?

How do these events occur?

This stage of study is like an investigator collecting evidence to construct a case. Study the scene of the crime, so to speak, gather all the evidence, and be careful not to overlook anything that is significant to the passage at hand. In the next step, you will examine the findings, so only concern yourself with highlighting key insights in the text at this stage. Remember to note as many facts as possible.

Explanation—What Does the Text Mean?

In the second step of the inductive process, you will study the facts that you gathered during the observation stage. Out of these facts, a scriptural truth will emerge. This truth, called a *theological principle,* is a summary of the same truth conveyed by the author to the original audience. In their book *Grasping God's Word,* Duvall and Hays outline five criteria that every theological principle must meet:

1. The principle should be clearly reflected in the text.
2. The principle should be timeless and not attached to a specific situation.
3. The principle should not be culturally bound.
4. The principle should correspond to the teaching of the rest of Scripture.
5. The principle should be relevant to both the biblical and the contemporary audience.[54]

As in the observation stage, ask the text a series of questions to help you arrive at its meaning. Here are a few questions that are helpful to me. Discerning the answers to these questions will help you discover the theological truth of any passage you are studying:

What do the key terms mean?

How do the verses or phrases relate to each other?

How does this passage fit into the larger story of the book it is in?

How does this passage relate to the story of the Bible as a whole?

How does this passage point to or speak of Jesus Christ?

What are the differences between the biblical audience and me?

As you study, remember that God inspired every word of Scripture. Each word is bursting with meaning. A good Bible dictionary, such as Harper's Bible Dictionary, is a valuable tool in understanding the words of Scripture. Focusing on the original words used rather than modern renderings of those words will assist you in determining the author's intended meaning.

Question to Consider

Why are observation and explanation essential in the interpretation process?

Application—How Does the Text Apply to Me?

The Bible is not merely a book to be learned, but a book to be lived. God has something to say to *you* through His Word, a truth that, when practiced faithfully, will make a difference in your life. This truth, called the application of a text, is the valuable payoff for all of your hard work in the first two steps.

When we apply the Bible, we focus God's truth upon our specific, life-related situations, helping us understand how to use what we have learned.[55] We must not be satisfied only with identifying key ideas from Scripture. We must proceed to discover how these truths apply to our lives. The goal of learning the Bible is not the accumulation of knowledge about the Bible. We must not study the Bible to merely learn facts to fill our minds, but to learn lessons to form our lives. In his epistle, James warned us of the danger of learning Scripture, but not applying it to our lives:

> *But be doers of the word, and not hearers only, deceiving yourselves. For if anyone is a hearer of the word and not a doer, he is like a man who looks intently at his natural face in a mirror. For he looks at himself and goes away and at once forgets what he was like. But the one who looks into the perfect law, the law of liberty, and perseveres, being no hearer who forgets but a doer who acts, he will be blessed in his doing.* (James 1:22–24)

Failing to apply God's Word to our lives and obey it is like a person who looks in a mirror, sees an imperfection, and walks away without taking care of it. What person sees food or dirt on his or her face and walks away without washing it off? Nobody who has even a trace of dignity would go on with a dirty face. Likewise, any person who cares for himself at all will seek what God's Word says and follow it. (Applying the Word and obeying the commands of Christ will be discussed at length in chapter 9.)

The transforming power of God's Word builds up our spiritual lives, providing motivation and guidance for pleasing God. However, this power—the power to affect spiritual growth—is released only when we correctly interpret the Bible.[56]

Our ultimate goal in studying the Bible is to become more like Christ. God works everything in our lives toward this end (Rom. 8:28–29). Therefore, it is essential that we apply what we learn in God's Word to making us more like Jesus.

Here are some questions to help you discover the application of a verse or passage of Scripture:

Is there an application already in the text?

Is there a command or exhortation for how we should live?

What does this biblical principle mean today?

What would the application of this verse look like in my life?

What difference does this make in my life?

How can this biblical principle help me in my walk with God?

As you study, do not forget that you need the Holy Spirit's help throughout this entire process. As stated earlier, He illuminates our minds and guides us into all the truth of Scripture. Be encouraged! You are not alone in your quest to know what God has to say to you. With the Holy Spirit's help, you *can* understand God's Word and put it to work in your life:

> *But the anointing that you received from him abides in you, and you have no need that anyone should teach you. But as his anointing teaches you about everything, and is true, and is no*

lie—just as it has taught you, abide in him. (1
John 2:27)

Questions to Consider
*What is the goal of application? What
are the dangers of misapplying a text?*

Spiritual Sleuths

Let's practice what we have learned by observing a
familiar passage of Scripture that has frequently been
misunderstood and misapplied. In his closing remarks
to the church at Philippi, the Apostle Paul stated,

> *"I can do all things through him who strength-
> ens me."* (Phil. 4:13)

Misinterpretation of Scripture often occurs when
we rush to apply a verse without understanding its context. Such is the case with this verse. It has been quoted
by people in every situation imaginable. Athletes seem
to be especially fond of claiming it in an attempt to har-
ness superhuman strength for their competitions. Is
this an appropriate use of this Scripture? Is this what
Paul really meant when he originally made this statement by inspiration of the Holy Spirit?

Start by reading Philippians 4:13 several times.
Then, identify the author of the book, as well as his
original audience. If this information is not readily
apparent, then you can easily find it by consulting
a Bible dictionary, a study Bible, or a commentary.
These invaluable resources are available at your local
Christian bookstore and for free online. Ask your pastor to recommend specific resources. In this case, we

have already provided this information: Paul wrote the book to the church at Philippi.

Next, identify the key words or phrases in the passage: *"all things," "through Him,"* and *"strengthens."* Now, establish the context in which Paul made this statement by zooming out to include the surrounding verses.

After observing everything possible about the text, proceed to step two: explain and interpret the facts about the passage. Why did the apostle say this? To what was he specifically referring when he said, "I can do all things"? Since the context of the entire passage defines the terms, read again the surrounding verses, this time more carefully:

> *I rejoiced in the Lord greatly that now at length you have revived your concern for me. You were indeed concerned for me, but you had no opportunity. Not that I am speaking of being in need, for I have learned in whatever situation I am to be content. I know how to be brought low, and I know how to abound. In any and every circumstance, I have learned the secret of facing plenty and hunger, abundance and need. I can do all things through him who strengthens me.* (Phil. 4:10–13)

Are there any statements in the preceding verses that shed light on the phrase "all things"? Indeed, there are. Paul had learned the invaluable secret of contentment in the school of hard knocks, suffering times of dire need in his life. He was as content when he had little as he was when he had much. This sets the stage for the term, *all things.* He puts a period on this point by adding the words, *through him* and *strengthens.*

Thus, we find that Paul is not making the same claim people often make when quoting this verse today. He is not claiming the ability to do anything and everything, without exception. He is not declaring that he possesses superhuman strength to defy all odds. Instead, he is disclosing that the source of his power is Christ. Christ strengthens him—gives him the power—to be content in every situation. His contentment is not dictated by his circumstances; it is found in His relationship with Christ. With Christ, he is happy with little, or with much. *All things* refers to whatever circumstances in which he found himself.

By stating that he can do all things through the One who strengthens him, Paul is saying that he is able to go without certain things when it is for the sake of Christ. Additionally, Paul hints at the fact that God gives us the ability to do without certain things that we usually categorize as needs. This is the interpretation of this verse.

How can we apply Philippians 4:13 today? The theological principle, created by building a bridge from the ancient world to the present world, could be, "The secret to contentment for Paul was his unwavering dependence on Christ." A practical application sentence might look like this statement: "When my focus is on Christ, I can endure any and every situation that may arise." Or, "I can thrive in any situation, because Christ, not worldly things, is the source of my strength."

Go For It!

By investing some time and energy in applying these steps to your Bible study, you will be well on your way to understanding exactly what God has to say to you through His amazing Word. As with any new skill, interpreting the Bible takes practice, so don't give up. The more you do it, the better you will become at it. Before long, you will begin reaping the dividends of your investment, and studying God's Word will become one of the most joyful activities of your life. You will soon find yourself saying with David,

"Oh how I love your [Word]! It is my meditation all the day." (Ps. 119:97)

Point to Ponder

Read John 14:14 and apply the principles concerning context to determine the application.

Memory Verse
2 Timothy 3:16–17

Chapter 7

C.L.O.S.E.R.
OBEY: FOLLOW THE LEADER

"If you love me, you will keep my commandments."
John 14:15

"If Christ is not Lord of all, he is not Lord at all."
C. T. Studd

Nineteenth-century philosopher Søren Kierkegaard told a parable of a community of ducks waddling off to duck church to hear the duck preacher. That particular morning, the duck preacher spoke eloquently about their God-given ability to fly. "With these wings," said the duck preacher, "there is nowhere you cannot go; there is no God-given task you cannot accomplish. With these wings, you can soar into the presence of God." Shouts of "Amen!" quacked throughout the duck congregation. After the service, the ducks left, commenting on what a wonderful message they had heard—as they waddled back home. Proclaiming the call to fly had done nothing to change the ducks.

This fable hits painfully close to home in today's churches. Unfortunately, many people attend church, sing the songs, hear a biblical message, leave the service, and return home the same way they left. There is no apparent change in their lives.

Dallas Willard began *The Great Omission* with a pertinent illustration: "If your neighbor is having trouble with his automobile, you might think he just got a lemon. And you might be right. But if you found that he was supplementing his gasoline with a quart of water now and then, you would not blame the car or its maker for it not running, or for running in fits and starts. You would say that the car was not built to work under the conditions imposed by the owner. And you would certainly advise him to put only the appropriate kind of fuel in the tank. After some restorative work, perhaps the car would then run fine."[57]

The church has been providing new believers with the wrong fuel for growth. In some cases, they've been providing no fuel at all. The problem is not with the Architect of the church, nor is it with His plan. The problem lies with leaders of His movement—namely, pastors—and their lack of emphasis on discipleship. Bill Hull, a leading author in the area of discipleship, stated, "I find it particularly puzzling that we struggle to put disciple-making at the center of ministry even though Jesus left us with the clear imperative to make disciples."[58]

Greatest Show on Earth

Between 22 and 10 BC, Herod constructed a mammoth amphitheater in the seacoast town of Caesarea, less than thirty miles from the birthplace of Christ. Supported by granite columns, this magnificent structure was the first of its kind, providing seating for 3,500 to 4,000 people (see Figure 2). While we cannot be sure, most historians assume that Jesus visited this town. Archeologists know that He at least knew of Herod's amphitheater.

If Jesus had been an American preacher, He would have seen a great opportunity presented by this colossal venue. The local media would have advertised the event as, "The Greatest Sermon on Earth. The lame will walk, the blind will see, the deaf will hear, and the dead will rise. Ladies and gentlemen, boys and girls, kids of all ages, come and meet God in the flesh—Jesus the Christ."[59] Jesus would have sent His disciples through the town with flyers in hand and instructions to place them on every chariot they could find. It would have been billed as the biggest revival the world had ever seen. If Jesus had carried out ministry like many of our pastors today, He would have packed the place with people every night for weeks. Cards would have been signed, hands would have been raised, and people would have walked the aisles.

Figure 2

But Jesus was not an American pastor. Although He spoke to large crowds on occasion, ministering to the masses was not Jesus's first priority. His foremost concern was twelve men. Yes, He spent his life training a dozen men to obey His commands.

Finished the Task

Unfortunately, obedience is not a priority for many professing believers today. Too many Christians have bought into the idea that Christianity is little more than reciting a prayer or making a decision to receive Jesus, in order to secure a position in heaven. A. W. Tozer believed that "a notable heresy has come into being throughout evangelical Christian circles—the widely accepted concept that we humans can choose to accept Christ only because we need Him as Savior and that we have the right to postpone our obedience to Him as Lord as long as we want to. . . . Salvation apart from obedience is unknown in the sacred Scripture."[60] Genuine, saving faith produces obedience to Christ's commands, including His command to make disciples.

On His way to the cross, Jesus prayed for His disciples—not only for the twelve, but also for all who would later follow Him. In His prayer, Jesus made a bold statement to His Father, saying, *"I glorified you on earth, having accomplished the work that you gave me to do"* (John 17:4). God had given Him a task to complete, and He confidently declared that He had finished it.

What was the work Jesus was given to do? Many would argue that Jesus was talking about dying on the cross. This, however, cannot be true, for His prayer preceded the crucifixion, and He could not then have described His work as having been accomplished. The context of the passage provides the correct answer. The work that Jesus was given to do was to train disciples.

The Lord's Prayer in John 17 is a powerful discourse on disciple-making.

In *The Lost Art of Discipleship,* Leroy Eims states, "When you read the prayer carefully, you'll notice that He did not mention miracles or multitudes, but forty times He referred to the men whom God had given Him out of the world."[61] Jesus invested in people, not programs. Yes, He spoke to the multitudes, but He spent His life with twelve men. Before leaving this earth, it was no coincidence that Jesus commanded His disciples to follow in His footsteps by making disciples: *"Go therefore and make disciples of all nations, baptizing them in the name of the Father and of the Son and of the Holy Spirit, teaching them to observe all that I have commanded you"* (Matt. 28:19–20).

How do you make disciples? By teaching them to obey His commands. In order to do so, you must first know His words yourself. You must get into the Word until the Word gets into you.

Questions to Consider

Why is Jesus's prayer in John 17 significant? How does this prayer affect your life as a believer?

To Know or Not to Know

Being a disciple, however, involves far more than gaining knowledge about God and the Bible. Many professing believers have read the entire Bible many times, and they have attended church and Sunday school for many years. Still, they are far from being

Christ's true disciples. They know the answers to all the questions in the Bible quiz, but they are missing the essence of following Christ. Discipleship is obedience to Christ's commands.

In his first epistle to the church, the apostle John wrote about the qualities that are evident in the life of a genuine Christian. We sometimes call these "the birthmarks of the believer." One of these prominent birthmarks is obedience to Christ:

> *And by this we know that we have come to know him, if we keep his commandments. Whoever says, "I know him" but does not keep his commandments is a liar, and the truth is not in him, but whoever keeps his word, in him truly the love of God is perfected. By this we may know that we are in him: whoever says he abides in him ought to walk in the same way in which he walked.* (1 John 2:3–6)

The word *know* saturates this text. In fact, John used this term thirty times in this letter alone. This word is not speaking of mental knowledge; that is, an awareness of facts or information. It means to have a personal, experiential knowledge of something through close interaction.

This type of knowledge is not something that an individual obtains once and for all, but it is the ongoing result of a personal encounter. It is the direct, first-hand understanding of something that can only be acquired through experiencing it.

The Classical Greeks believed that human reason gives us this knowledge. The Hellenistic Greeks suggested that this knowledge comes through secret religions, such as Gnosticism. The Hebrews taught that this knowledge was obtained only through revelation of God's truth. The Bible teaches that God reveals

Himself and His truth to us when we personally and regularly spend time communing with Him.

When Jesus said, *"And you will know the truth, and the truth will set you free"* (John 8:32), He was not referring to gathering information or data. He was speaking of this intimate knowledge that comes only through a deep, personal relationship with Him. He is the *truth* (John 14:6).

The corresponding Hebrew word for this intimate, experiential knowledge is used throughout the Old Testament to describe the sexual oneness of a husband and wife. For example, *"Adam knew Eve his wife, and she conceived and bore Cain"* (Gen. 4:1). Just as intimacy is enriched through spending time with your spouse, this knowledge comes through uninterrupted, unhindered time with God. It is this personal knowledge that is the basis of discipleship, and it involves more than reading the Bible, memorizing Scripture, and praying. It is intimately walking in communion with the Father through living, loving, and spending time with God.

If this intimate knowledge could be transmitted instantly, Jesus would have placed His hands on the apostles' heads and ordered, "Know the truth." Instead, He said, *"You shall know the truth,"* instructing them that knowing Him is a process, the process of practicing the principles of the Bible in the walk of everyday life.

You might be saying, "This chapter is about obeying God. Why the long dissertation on knowledge?" Because *knowing God is the foundation for obeying Him*. Did you catch it? Look again at what John wrote:

> *And by this we know that we have come to know Him, if we keep His commandments.* (1 John 2:3)

John was simply repeating what he had learned directly from Jesus. In his outstanding explanation of John 15, Warren Wiersbe points out that Jesus taught that the secret of obeying Him is loving Him (John 15:9–10), and the secret of loving Him is *knowing* Him (John 15:15).[62] Wiersbe directly stated, "It all begins with your knowing Christ in a deeper way."[63]

Ezra is an Old Testament model of obedience. In Ezra 7:10, we find these words: *"For Ezra had set his heart to study the Law of the LORD, and to do it."* He intentionally purposed not only to set aside time to study God's Word, but to act upon what he learned. Similarly, Jesus concluded the Great Commission in Matthew 28 with these words, "Teach them to *obey* all that I have commanded you" (emphasis mine). Jesus does not expect His followers merely to listen, hear, or take notes of His teachings, as helpful as these principles are; He expects us to obey His Word.

Dave Browning, in *Deliberate Simplicity*, stated, "We are convinced that the gap holding back most believers is not the gap between what they know and what they don't know. It's the gap between what they know and what they're living. *Many Christians are . . . educated beyond their obedience* (emphasis mine)."[64] Most Christians do not need to attend another Bible study to grow in their relationship with the Lord. They need to start living what they have already learned. Mark Twain said it best, "It's not the things in the Bible that I *don't* understand that bother me. It's the things in the Bible that I *do* understand that bother me" (emphasis mine).[65] Stop wondering about what you don't know, and start obeying the things you do.

Questions to Consider

What is the difference between the knowledge of God and knowing God? How does your answer affect the way you act / live / behave?

Great Expectations

Jesus expected His disciples to follow His example of commitment to the Father. Luke recorded Jesus's interaction with three men on the roadside (Luke 9:57–62). With misguided expectations, the first potential follower assumed Jesus was a superstar rabbi who enjoyed the luxuries of the best hotels. But Jesus sharply corrected his self-serving view, replying, "Foxes have holes, and birds of the air have nests, but the Son of Man has nowhere to lay his head" (Luke 9:58).

Because of misplaced priorities, a second would-be disciple was willing to follow Jesus only after his father died. Recognizing this man's desire to receive his inheritance rather than forsake all for the Kingdom of God, Jesus sternly answered, *"Leave the dead to bury their own dead. But as for you, go and proclaim the kingdom of God"* (Luke 9:59).

Finally, a third man approached Jesus. On the surface, his request appeared sincere. "Jesus," he said, "I will follow you, but first let me say farewell to my parents." Seeing through the man's empathetic words to the real motive of his heart, Jesus tersely replied, *"No one who puts his hand to the plow and looks back is fit for the kingdom of God"* (Luke 9:61–62).

All three encounters enforce the same point: Jesus must be first in your life. He will never settle for second place. He demands unwavering commitment. You must love Him supremely, above everyone and everything else.

Question to Consider

List the three roadblocks to following Jesus in Luke 9:57–62. What roadblocks impede your relationship with Christ?

Who Says?

The stages of obeying the Lord can be illustrated by a triangle:

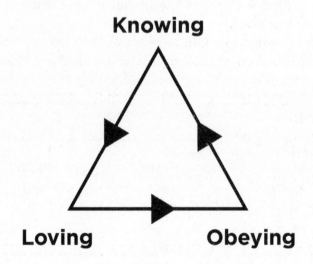

Figure 3

Notice how it works: the progression flows from knowing God to loving Him. The more we love Him, the more we desire to obey Him. The more we obey Him, the more He reveals Himself to us. Then we love Him even more, which causes us to obey Him better, which prompts God to reveal more of Himself to us. It is a continuing process.

Remember, you will never serve Him faithfully until you love Him fervently.

When you love God enough to obey Him, He will respond by showering His blessings upon you. Here are a few promises from the Word:

- You will have assurance of salvation (1 John 2:5).
- God's love will be perfected in you (1 John 2:5).
- You will be successful (Josh. 1:8).
- Your prayers will be answered (John 15:7).
- You will enjoy friendship with Christ (John 15:14).
- Your needs will be met (Matt. 6:33).
- God will direct your path in life (Prov. 3:5–6).

Questions to Consider

Describe the relationship between knowing, loving, and obeying God. Does this motivate you to study the Bible? If so, how?

Undisciplined Disciples

In *Spiritual Disciplines for the Christian Life*, Donald Whitney wrote, "So many professing Christians are so spiritually undisciplined that they seem to have little fruit and power in their lives. I've seen men and women who discipline themselves for the purpose of excelling in their profession, but discipline themselves minimally for the purpose of godliness. I've seen Christians who are faithful to the church of God, who frequently demonstrate genuine enthusiasm for the things of God, and who dearly love the Word of God, trivialize their effectiveness for the Kingdom of God through lack of discipline. Spiritually they are a mile wide and an inch deep. There are not deep, time-worn channels of communing discipline between them and God. They have dabbled in everything but disciplined themselves in nothing."[66]

Rig and Ryder, my two sons, learned how to play Simon Says at a young age. It became Kandi's favorite game, because Simon always said to clean up the toy room before bedtime. You remember the rules: The leader tells you to do something by beginning an order with, "Simon Says." "Simon says jump." You jump. "Simon says raise your hands." You raise your hands. Then, when you least expect it, the person calling the commands abruptly barks, "Sit down," without first saying, "Simon says." Without thinking, you sit down, and lose the game.

It's amazing how well we followed rules as a child when Simon said them, but how do you respond when Jesus says _____? We follow the rules of a silly game, yet at times, we ignore the commands of the One who loves us and gave Himself for us.

Jesus issued many commands for us to follow. Don't overlook His last—and most crucial—one:

"Make disciples!"

Point to Ponder

Think about areas of your life that need to be submitted to the Lordship of Christ.

Memory Verse
2 John 1:6

 *Chapter 8*

C.L.O.S.E.R.

STORE: AN ETERNAL INVESTMENT STRATEGY

"I have stored up your word in my heart,
that I might not sin against you."
Psalm 119:11

"I know of no other single practice in the Christian
life more rewarding, practically speaking, than
memorizing Scripture. . . . No other single exercise
pays greater spiritual dividends! Your prayer life will
be strengthened. Your witnessing will be sharper
and much more effective. Your attitudes and out-
look will begin to change. Your mind will become
alert and observant. Your confidence and assurance
will be enhanced. Your faith will be solidified."
Chuck Swindoll

As unbelievable as it sounds, ultra-Orthodox Jews
committed the entire Babylonian Talmud—all 5,422
pages of it—to memory. You read that right. A pin
could be stuck into any of the sixty-three sections, and
they could recite every word on every page.[67]

The art of memorization is quickly becoming a thing of the past. In the first century, however, memorization was critical. In an age when the only way to store and transmit material was to copy it by hand, men and women had to commit information to memory. Imagine waking up tomorrow to a world without written words. Life as we know it would come to a screeching halt, because we depend on electronic sources for practically all of our information. Few people these days can quickly recall phone numbers of family members or friends. For that matter, some cannot recall their *own* phone number without checking. I know that we live in such a time. That is why the doctrine of Scripture memorization is more important than ever.

In most churches, memorizing verses of the Bible is a task reserved for the children. Once a child moves into "big church," the discipline of Scripture memorization goes out the window. It is difficult to persuade most church members to *read* the Bible on a daily basis, much less memorize it.

But for the believer who truly desires to be a full-fledged follower of Christ, simply reading the Bible daily will not be enough. As a disciple, your goal is not merely to get into the Word, but to get the Word into you. Earnest disciples take seriously Paul's exhortation to *"let the word of Christ dwell in you richly"* (Col. 3:16).

For God's Word to dwell in you, you must memorize it. How many times have you read a page of a book and quickly forgotten what you read? True learning comes from that which is memorized.

The study of the human memory is a most fascinating and invaluable topic. Scientific research has established that practically all of what we read passes through the short-term memory, which acts like a filter for the massive amount of information we encounter on a daily basis. In contrast, the long-term memory can hold an infinite amount of information. The more that a piece of information is repeated, the higher the probability is that it will be retained in the long-term memory. Repetition is the key to learning.

Therefore, if an individual wants to preserve something in the long-term memory, he or she must take an intentional step to retain it. Only two options have stood the test of time and experience: repetition and intentional memorization.

How do you remember a phone number? Either by dialing it frequently enough that, over a period of time, it is stamped upon your long-term memory; or by intentionally memorizing it. Which of those do you think is faster?

I have a friend who can quote nearly all of the book of Philippians—not because he has intentionally memorized it, but because it is his favorite book of the Bible, and he reads it in its entirety every week. Some of you are undoubtedly thinking, *"That's* the way to do it? Memorizing is a chore." But guess how long he has been reading Philippians every week?

Twenty-six years! That's over 1,350 times!

If you are not intentionally memorizing God's Word, you are missing out on one of the most valuable blessings of the Christian life. I want to encourage you, motivate you, beg you to make memorizing the Word of God a top priority and regular practice in your life. Nothing will do more to help you gain victory over your spiritual enemies—the world, the flesh, and the devil—than faithfully practicing this discipline.

Memorization and Meditation

The spiritual discipline of meditation is mentioned far more in Scripture than is memorization. God informed Joshua that the secret of success is meditating on God's Word:

> *This Book of the Law shall not depart from your mouth, but you shall meditate on it day and night, so that you may be careful to do according to all that is written in it. For then you will make your way prosperous, and then you will have good success.* (Josh. 1:8)

Meditation on the Word is also the key to blessing, prosperity, and fruitfulness:

> *Blessed is the man who walks not in the counsel of the wicked, nor stands in the way of sinners, nor sits in the seat of scoffers; but his delight is in the law of the LORD, and on his law he meditates day and night. He is like a tree planted by streams of water that yields its fruit in its season, and its leaf does not wither. In all that he does, he prospers.* (Ps. 1:1–3)

Psalm 119, the longest chapter in the Bible, is David's declaration of his love for God's Word. Each of its 176 verses is about the Bible. In a number of those verses, David speaks of how meditating on God's Word has changed his life.

Joshua Foer, U.S. Memory Champion, wrote, "The ancient and medieval way of reading was totally different from how we read today. One didn't just memorize texts; one ruminated on them—chewed them up and regurgitated them like cud—and in the process, became intimate with them in a way that made them one's own. As Petrarch said in a letter to a friend, 'I ate in the morning what I would digest in the evening; I swallowed as a boy what I would ruminate upon as an older man. I have thoroughly absorbed these writings, implanting them not only in my memory but in my marrow.' Augustine was said to be so steeped in the Psalms that they, as much as Latin itself, comprised the principle language in which he wrote."[68]

What Foer describes is exactly what Scripture means by meditation. Most people associate meditation with New Age practices such as yoga, transcendental meditation, relaxation techniques, or other exercises that quiet the mind with the goal of the spirit transcending the body.

When I was a new believer, just a few months old in the faith, I was invited to attend a spiritual, New Age retreat. Although my Bible knowledge was limited, *spiritual* was a word I was familiar with, so I accepted the invitation.

When I arrived, an odd assortment of New Age practitioners introduced themselves to me. Included in these "experts" were Reiki masters, Gregorian chanters, breath work instructors, teachers of transcendental meditation, clairvoyant readers, astrologists, and others offering instruction on how to free the spiritual person from the physical body.

As an unlearned, immature believer, I practiced the techniques that I was taught at the retreat for the next three months. Every night, I sat in total silence in my bedroom, eyes shut, legs folded, arms extended with forefinger and thumb touching.

The goal of this exercise was finding the solutions to all of my problems and the answers to all of my questions within my soul, through meditation and silence. I could accomplish this, according to the retreat teachers, through relaxing—quieting the ripples of my soul in order that knowledge, happiness, and peace could emerge.

But it just didn't work for me. Every session yielded the same result. I would wake up a few hours later after having fallen asleep on the floor. Apparently, I relaxed a little too much.

When I started reading the Bible, I quickly realized that this type of meditation was unbiblical. Romans 7:18 supports this: *"For I know that nothing good dwells in me, that is, in my flesh."* I learned that if I tried, in and of myself, to find answers, I would always find the wrong answers. In order to find truth, we must look outside of ourselves—to Christ (John 14:6). Looking within ourselves is not biblical meditation.

Biblical meditation is not turning off the lights and spending hours pondering nothingness. It is not mental passivity, but, rather, focused mental activity. Through meditation, a believer focuses on the Word, ponders the Word, savors the Word, and delights in the Word.

The Hebrew word for *meditate* means "to murmur or mutter." Old Testament Jews thought in pictures, so the author of the first Psalm used the image of a pigeon cooing. Imagine the noise this bird makes over and over. This is the picture the Scripture draws of a person meditating: murmuring the Scriptures over and over in one's mind, or even aloud. In Israel, it is not uncommon to observe a Jewish rabbi walking with his head down, talking to himself. He's not crazy; he is reciting from memory a portion of the Torah.

Scriptural meditation is difficult without memorization. Before the Word can become a part of your being, you must first implant it in your memory. Memorizing God's Word affords you the opportunity to contemplate God's Word anytime and anywhere, to chew on it until it becomes a part of you.

Points to Ponder

Read Psalm 1:1–4. Identify the benefits of meditation. Consider how these benefits will impact your daily walk with Christ.

Bible Brew

Memorizing Scripture saturates your life with God's Word. In *Spiritual Disciplines for the Christian Life,* Donald Whitney illustrates the effect of memorizing the Word with a cup of hot tea. Whitney explains, "You are the cup of hot water and the intake of Scripture is represented by the tea bag. Hearing God's Word is like one dip of the tea bag into the cup. Some of the tea's flavor is absorbed by the water, but not as much as would occur with a more thorough soaking of the bag." He adds, "In this analogy, reading, studying, and memorizing God's Word are represented by additional plunges of the tea bag into the cup. The more frequently the tea enters the water, the more effect it has."[69]

As the flavor of the tea dissolves into the water until its color reflects a reddish tint, so should our lives be saturated with the Word until we are distinctively marked by the infusion of Scripture.

> ### Point to Ponder
>
> *With the "tea bag" analogy in mind,*
> *think about what steps need to take place*
> *for the Word to saturate your life.*

A Mind-Altering Experience

While reading the Bible opens our spiritual ears to hear from God, Scripture memorization injects our minds with what He says. Colossians 3:2 states, *"Set your mind on things that are above, not on things that are on earth."* The New Living Translation renders the verse, *"Let heaven fill your thoughts."* When we saturate our minds with the Word of God, it permeates our entire person, everything we say and do. Our sinful minds are cleansed as the water of God's Word flows through them, flushing out the corrupt thoughts of our old nature, and replacing them with the pure, undefiled ways of God (John 15:3; Eph. 5:26). As a result, our lives are transformed:

> *Do not be conformed to this world, but be transformed by the renewal of your mind, that by testing you may discern what is the will of God, what is good and acceptable and perfect.* (Rom. 12:2)

By renewing our minds with the infusion of God's Word, we focus our attention on godly principles. Our lives will begin to look less like the world and more like Christ. Paul taught this principle to the church at Colossae:

Do not lie to one another, seeing that you have put off the old self with its practices and have put on the new self, which is being renewed in knowledge after the image of its creator. (Col. 3:9–10)

The Greek word for renewal can also be translated as *renovation*. What do we do when we renovate something? We tear down that which is old and deteriorated, and we rebuild it with that which is new and solid. This is exactly what happens when we fill our minds with God's Word. Our darkened, corrupt minds are replaced with the mind of the Lord. Therefore, as Paul teaches in Romans 12:2, we are able to confidently discern God's will for our lives. In fact, the Bible teaches us that, with the indwelling Holy Spirit guiding us into the truths of His Word, we have the mind of Christ. Therefore, we can understand the mind of the Lord (1 Cor. 2:16). We can know God's will for our lives (Col. 1:9), understand it (Col. 1:9), and actually test or prove it (Rom. 12:2).

The Benefits Are Tremendous

When you bury the treasure of God's Word in your heart, the Holy Spirit will bring it to mind when you need it most. Don't just take my word for it. Try it for yourself. You will be amazed at how it will affect your life. As you continue to memorize and meditate upon God's Word, you will find that the benefits are endless. Here are just a few:

1. Meditation and memorization keep you from sin.

   I have stored up Your Word in my heart, that I might not sin against You. (Ps. 119:11)

2. Meditation and memorization transform your thinking.

   Do not be conformed to this world, but be transformed by the renewal of your mind. (Rom. 12:2)

3. Meditation and memorization equip you to share your testimony.

   But in your hearts honor Christ the Lord as holy, always being prepared to make a defense to anyone who asks you for a reason for the hope that is in you. (1 Pet. 3:15)

4. Meditation and memorization provide direction for your life.

   Your Word is a lamp unto my feet and a light unto my path. (Ps. 119:105)

5. Meditation and memorization produce spiritual growth in your life.

   And now I commend you to God and to the word of His grace, which is able to build you up and to give you the inheritance among all those who are sanctified. (Acts 20:32)

6. Meditation and memorization equip you to fight temptation.

   And the tempter came and said to him, "If you are the Son of God, command these stones to become loaves of bread." But he answered, "It is written, Man shall not live by bread alone, but by every

word that comes from the mouth of God."
(Matt. 4:3–4)

This short list is just the beginning of what God's powerful Word can do when we invest the effort to hide it in our hearts. Your list will continually grow as you march on in your journey of faith, encouraging you to memorize more and more of the Bible.

Armed for Battle

Meditating on and memorizing God's Word will increase your capacity to obey what you know. What you put in your mind will alter your environment. Our minds are the battleground of spiritual warfare, and spiritual battles must be fought with spiritual weapons. Paul explained this to the church at Corinth:

> *For though we walk in the flesh, we are not waging war according to the flesh. For the weapons of our warfare are not of the flesh but have divine power to destroy strongholds. We destroy arguments and every lofty opinion raised against the knowledge of God, and take every thought captive to obey Christ. (2 Cor. 10:3–5)*

What is our spiritual weapon? God has armed us with the *"sword of the Spirit, which is the word of God"* (Eph. 6:17). The Bible is powerful, sharper than even a deadly, double-edged sword. It is capable of piercing through your innermost being and separating every impure thought out of your heart and mind:

> *For the word of God is living and active, sharper than any two-edged sword, piercing to the division of soul and of spirit, of joints and of marrow, and discerning the thoughts and intentions of the heart. (Heb. 4:12)*

145

Simple Steps

Some people do struggle with memorization, and many feel that they cannot memorize God's Word. Others want to meditate on God's Word, but don't know where to start, or specifically what to do. Here is a simple system that will help with both memorization and meditation:

Picture It: What does this spiritual truth look like? Visualize what the text is saying in your mind. Picture it as a reality in your life.

Ponder It: To use an old expression, mull it over. Think on it. Repeat it over and over to yourself. What does this text mean? What do the individual words mean? What is God trying to express?

Personalize It: What does it mean specifically in your life? What does this look like in your life? What actions need to happen for the truth to become a reality?

Pray Over It: Ask God to bring this truth to life in your everyday experience. Ask Him to make the truth real, and to reveal how you should respond.

Walking Point

Take a second look at Psalm 1 with this four-fold method for meditation. Did you understand the text in a deeper way? How so?

Storing Up Treasure

If you search, you'll find hundreds of methods for memorizing Scripture. While each is effective in its own right, one simple system has been effective for me. All you need is a pack of index cards and a committed desire to memorize God's Word.

It's easy. Write the reference of the verse on one side of the card and the text of the verse on the other (see Appendix 6 for an example). Focus on five verses at a time, and carry your pack of Scripture cards with you.

Throughout the day, whenever you have a few minutes, pull out your pack of Scripture cards and review them. Read the reference first, followed by the verse. Continue to recite the verse until you get a feel for the flow of the passage. When you are comfortable with the text, look only at the reference side of the card in order to test your recall.

It is important to recite the reference first, then the verse, and finish with the reference again. This will prevent you from becoming a concordance cripple. As a new believer, I was forced to look up every verse in the concordance at the back of my Bible. Sometimes, when I quoted a passage, the person would ask me, "Where did you get that?" I could only respond, "Somewhere in the Bible." By memorizing the references, you will speak with authority and gain the respect of your hearers when you quote Scripture.

When you master five verses, begin to study five more. Review all of the verses you have learned at least once a week. As your pack grows, you will be encouraged to keep going in Scripture memorization, and you will experience its powerful effects in your life.

A Labor of Love

A lady in a small town manicured a picturesque garden in the front of her house. Every day as they drove or strolled by, her neighbors admired her beautiful creation. One day, when she was mulching her rose bed, a passerby commented, "You must have a green thumb."

Without hesitation she replied, "No. I have a purple thumb and two bruised knees."

Hard work is required to produce a beautiful garden, and it is equally necessary to memorize Scripture. Memorizing anything is not easy, which is why so many believers know so few Scriptures.

When we get to heaven, God is not going to be impressed with how many sports statistics we know by heart, how many television shows we can recall, or how many words of popular songs we can recite. But He will be overjoyed with our efforts to commit His life-changing Word to memory. When we hide His Word in our hearts, we are saying to God, "Your Word is important to me."

One time, I heard this one: "I am just too old to memorize Scripture."

My response to them was, "I would rather you spend one year working on one verse than to stand before Christ with none of His Word memorized."

Even though it is difficult, will you invest the time needed to hide God's Word in your heart? Will you put aside the computer, the Internet, and television to spend time pondering Scripture? Thomas Watson, Puritan pastor and teacher, commented, "The reason we come away so cold from reading the Word is because we do not warm ourselves at the fire of meditation."[70]

Question to Consider

List barriers that have prevented you from memorizing Scripture in the past. What steps will you take in order to remove these barriers?

Start Where?

Many people ask the same questions regarding Scripture memorization: "What verses should I memorize?" or, "Where do I begin?" A program called "Fighter Verses" has been helpful to me. A quick search through your app store will find it. This app takes the guesswork out by highlighting applicable memory verses for every week of the year (you can find it at http://fighterverses.com).

The best way to continue with the discipline of Scripture memory is with an accountability partner. Few people will consistently memorize unless they are accountable to someone. One of the advantages of a discipleship group is the built-in accountability system for Scripture memorization. By reciting passages weekly, group members will come prepared to quote their memorized verses. What gets measured, gets done.

If you are not in a discipleship group, get in one. If you cannot find a group, start one. This book will teach you how. At the least, ask someone to be your partner in memorizing Scripture. By doing so, you will not only help yourself, but the other individual as well.

The average Christian can quote few verses. Sadly, many can recite only John 3:16, along with the shortest verse in the Bible, *"Jesus wept"* (John 11:35).

Even more sadly, I believe Jesus could weep today because many of His so-called disciples have committed little, if any, of His Word to memory. Pause now to purpose that this will not be true of you, and to pray that God will help you to make the discipline of Scripture memory a priority in your life.

Walking Point

Consider memorizing a chapter of a book of the Bible, e.g., Psalm 1, Romans 8, John 15, Galatians 5, or Ephesians 2.

Memory Verse
Psalm 1:1–2

 *Chapter 9*

C.L.O.S.E.R.
EVANGELIZE: SHOW AND TELL

"Go into all the world and proclaim
the gospel to the whole creation."
Mark 16:15

"Evangelism is not a professional job for a few trained
men, but is instead the unrelenting responsibility of
every person who belongs to the company of Jesus."
Elton Trueblood

One of my most meaningful possessions is a picture
that hangs behind the desk in my office. I purchased
it in 2005, shortly after Kandi and I were married, but
that is not what makes it so special to me.

The picture is unique. At first glance, it appears
to be an ordinary picture of the Last Supper. Upon a
closer look, however, you discover that the images are
actually the words of John 13–16, cleverly highlighted
through creative typography. But the fact that the picture is crafted from the words of our Lord is not what
makes it unique to me.

When our home was destroyed by Hurricane Katrina in 2005, this picture was the only work of art that survived. That's why this print means so much to me.

Sharing the gospel is much like providing the backstory to that picture. Our lives ought to display God's work in us, just like that painting displayed its artist's incredible craftsmanship. But it is one thing to display the gospel through our lives. It is quite another to open our mouths and share why it is significant to us, that is, what it means to us—something that can change the destiny of others around us.

No matter how long we are saved, and how much we grow in our walk, we will never move beyond the gospel: the good news that Christ died for our sins, was buried, and rose again (1 Cor. 15:1–4). It is the sole basis for all that we are, all that we are becoming, and all that we will be. Every day, we are blessed because of God's great love for us, a love that He demonstrated by giving His Son to die in our place (Rom. 5:8). As we grow in discipleship, we gain a greater awareness of and appreciation for what Christ did for us on the cross. Indeed, our Savior defined discipleship as taking up our cross, and following His example of sacrifice, service, and selflessness (Luke 9:23).

Evangelism and discipleship are two oars attached to one boat. With only one oar in the water, you will go in a circle. Both oars are necessary to reach your destination. Both are essential to carrying out the Great Commission.

The gospel is received through evangelism and lived out through discipleship. Evangelism without discipleship will end when the evangelist dies. Likewise, discipleship without evangelism will cease when the disciple-maker dies. Derwin Gray, pastor of Transformational Church, states, "If our churches are not evangelistic, then our discipleship process has not been holistic."[71] True disciples make disciples, and disciples cannot be made without evangelism. It is a "both/and" rather than an "either/or" proposition.

The Secret of Success

Simply stated, evangelism is sharing the person and work of Christ to sinful human beings with the hope that they will repent of their sins and put their trust in Jesus as Savior and Lord.

In his classic book *The Master Plan of Evangelism*, Robert Coleman described Jesus's plan for reaching the world with the message of the gospel: "His concern was not with programs to reach the multitudes, but with men whom the multitudes would follow. . . . Men were to be his method of winning the world to God."[72] To put it bluntly, God's plan for reaching the world with the gospel revolves around *you*.

All four men who wrote inspired accounts of the life of Christ recorded His command to share the gospel:

All authority in heaven and on earth has been given to Me. Go therefore and make disciples of all nations, baptizing them in the name of the Father and of the Son and of the Holy Spirit, teaching them to observe all that I have commanded you. And behold, I am with you always, to the end of the age. (Matt. 28:18–20)

Go into all the world and proclaim the gospel to the whole creation. (Mark 16:15)

Repentance and forgiveness of sins should be proclaimed in His name to all nations, beginning from Jerusalem. (Luke 24:47)

*Peace be with you. As the Father has sent Me,
even so I am sending you.* (John 20:21)

While every scriptural account of Christ's time on
earth ends with this command, the book of Acts begins
with it:

*But you will receive power when the Holy Spirit
has come upon you, and you will be My witnesses
in Jerusalem and in all Judea and Samaria,
and to the end of the earth.* (Acts 1:8)

Acts is the story of how the handful of men in whom
Jesus invested His life obeyed this command, reaching
the world with the gospel.

Point to Ponder

*The departing words of Jesus in
Matthew 28:19 begin with the word
"go," which literally means "as you are
going." Think about your daily and
weekly routine. "As you are going,"
who can you share the gospel with?*

The Success is in the Sharing

Some people get the wrong idea about evangelism
by thinking that success is determined by how many
people we personally win to Christ. This is not the
teaching of Scripture. Success in evangelism is in the
sharing, not the *saving.* Only God can save, but He
commands us to share. Our responsibility begins and

ends with the sharing of the gospel. Paul made this crystal-clear to the carnal congregation at Corinth:

> *For when one says, "I am of Paul," and another, "I am of Apollos," are you not carnal? Who then is Paul, and who is Apollos, but ministers through whom you believed, as the Lord gave to each one? I planted, Apollos watered, but God gave the increase. So then neither he who plants is anything, nor he who waters, but God who gives the increase.* (1 Cor. 3:4–7 NKJV)

One of the challenges for us, a people influenced by a culture of success, is that we are programmed to measure results by counting converts for the sake of reporting numbers or boasting in results. By no means am I suggesting that we shouldn't keep records of the men and women who profess Christ. We must know who they are in order to point them toward baptism and move them into disciple-making groups. As many have correctly said, "We count people because people count." Somebody counted the number of people who believed on the Day of Pentecost.

But we must avoid the trap of counting converts to strike more notches on our spiritual belts or insert more feathers in our evangelistic caps. We don't get the credit for that. God alone saves, not us.

If numbers alone signified the success of ministry, William Carey's first years of ministry in India were a total failure. He didn't see *any* converts for seven years—not a single one. Adoniram Judson labored for six years in Burma before a single believer was identified. Were these faithful missionaries failures? By no means. God evaluates our faithfulness to share the gospel. He, and He alone, produces its fruit (John 15:4).

Bill Bright, the founder of Campus Crusade for Christ, captured it best: "Success in witnessing is simply taking the initiative to share Christ in the power of the Holy Spirit, and leaving the results to God."[73] That's true evangelistic success.

Regeneration, Not Reformation

Instead of focusing only on the word *conversion*, let's use the word *regeneration* in referring to salvation. This often ignored word is crucial in understanding our quest to see people come to Christ. Theologian Wayne Grudem defines regeneration as "a work of God in which He imparts spiritual life to us."[74] What role do you and I play in this work of regeneration? None whatsoever. It is entirely the work of God. Notice the pronoun God used in describing the work of regeneration:

> *I will give you a new heart, and a new spirit I will put within you. And I will remove the heart of stone from your flesh and give you a heart of flesh. And I will put My Spirit within you, and cause you to walk in My statutes and be careful to obey My rules.* (Ezek. 36:26–27)

This concept is also communicated at the beginning of John's Gospel:

> *But to all who did receive Him, who believed in His name, He gave the right to become children of God, who were born, not of blood nor of the will of the flesh nor of the will of man, but of God.* (John 1:12–13)

When I first moved to Chattanooga, Tennessee, I planted two crab apple trees in my backyard. At the end of the first season, one tree had budded and produced lush leaves. The other looked like Charlie Brown's Christmas tree, sporting a few stray twigs and diseased leaves.

The next year, I decided to give more attention to these trees. I fertilized the ground and spent a small fortune installing a timed watering system in the backyard. My evenings were consumed with pulling weeds, tilling soil, and killing bugs. I waited patiently for the trees to bud, only to have the second year repeat itself with one lush tree and one "Charlie Brown" scrawny collection of twigs.

After some investigation, I learned that the Charlie Brown tree was hopelessly diseased. Nothing could be done for it. The only solution was to rip the tree out of the ground and plant a completely new one in its place. Attempting to fix the tree by purchasing new soil, pulling up the weeds, tilling the ground, adding fertilizer, and saturating the ground with water would never produce healthy leaves. For all practical purposes, it was a dead tree.

Similarly, lost sinners are spiritually diseased because they are spiritually dead. All attempts to reform people through conventional, moralistic practices cannot bring about a new life. Even in the best possible soils, with the best possible tending, unbelievers are still spiritually dead.

When we believe upon Christ, God gives us a new life, which is exactly the meaning of regeneration. We are a new creation in Christ (2 Cor. 5:17). Paul vividly expressed this in his letter to the church at Ephesus:

> *And you were dead in the trespasses and sins in which you once walked, following the course of this world, following the prince of the power of the air, the spirit that is now at work in the sons of disobedience— among whom we all once lived in the passions of our flesh, carrying out the desires of the body and the mind, and were by nature children of wrath, like the rest of mankind. But God,*

being rich in mercy, because of the great love with which he loved us, even when we were dead in our trespasses, made us alive together with Christ— by grace you have been saved. (Eph. 2:1–5)

Birth, whether the first (physical) or the second (spiritual), is the exclusive work of God. God is the author of salvation, not us. God is the One who gives life to human beings, not us. And God is the One who sustains life, not us. Whenever we start taking credit for the results of evangelism, we are entering a slippery slope of pride and error.

At this point, many might say, "If God is the One who regenerates lost sinners, then maybe I don't need to participate in the process at all. I can just sit back and watch God do all the work."

Nothing could be farther from the truth. The sovereign work of God in salvation is not a license for laziness. God has challenged us to go and tell others about His love and grace. Like postal carriers on a mail route, our duty is to deliver the mail (the gospel) without messing with the package.

Point to Ponder

How does a bette understanding of the doctrine of regeneration motivate you to share the gospel?

Do You Know Me?

When I was in college, I signed up in a multilevel marketing business that offered telecommunication services. At nineteen years old, I quickly moved up the network ladder because I had memorized an effective marketing spiel: "If the money was right and it fit into your time schedule, would you be interested in looking at a serious business opportunity?" Who could say no to that?

However, my slick presentation was not effective with everyone. Some astute people recognized right away that the pitch was rehearsed. Many potential business associates were turned off because I came across as impersonal.

Similarly, the days of approaching people with a rehearsed, evangelistic "spiel" are numbered. The information age has birthed a generation of young people who can spot a fake a mile away. People today want to know you care about them before they listen to what you have to share. Integrity is expected.[75] With today's generation, you must earn the right to share the gospel by developing a relationship with them.

In the past, the church has viewed lost people as projects. We must reject this attitude and see people the way Jesus sees them.

Jesus Christ, without any sort of evangelistic spiel, shared the gospel through relationships. He met people where they were and cared about them for who they were. In John 3, Jesus met Nicodemus in the middle of the night. In John 4, Jesus spoke to the woman at the well. And in John 5, He ministered to a man who helplessly lay at the pool of Bethesda. We must first show people that we love them and care about them, and that they are not just another religious project (Appendix 8 contains seven avenues for building relationships with others).

Speak to Me

"Go into the world and preach the gospel. If necessary, use words."

Many of us are familiar with this famous quote, which is usually credited to St. Francis of Assisi. (By the way, historians believe that he didn't actually say this.)[76] It is another example of a popular statement that is unbiblical. Paul clearly stated that the gospel *must* be shared with words:

> For "everyone who calls on the name of the Lord will be saved." How then will they call on Him in whom they have not believed? And how are they to believe in Him of whom they have never heard? And how are they to hear without someone preaching? And how are they to preach unless they are sent? As it is written, "How beautiful are the feet of those who preach the good news. . . . So faith comes from hearing, and hearing through the word of Christ. (Rom. 10:13–15, 17)

Since the gospel is conveyed with words, we must present it in a way that is easily and clearly understood. In *What is the Gospel?*, Greg Gilbert explained the gospel with four simple words: God, Man, Christ, and Response. Mark Dever, a mentor of Gilbert's, expands upon this outline in his book *The Gospel and Personal Evangelism*: "The one and only God, who is holy, made us in his image to know him. But we sinned and cut ourselves off from him. In his great love, God became a man in Jesus, lived a perfect life and died on the cross, thus fulfilling the law himself and taking on himself the punishment for the sins of all those who would ever turn and trust in him. He rose again from the dead, showing that God accepts Christ's sacrifice and that God's wrath against us had been exhausted. He now calls us to repent of our sins and to trust in Christ alone for our forgiveness. If we repent of our sins and trust in Christ, we are born again into a new life, an eternal life with God."[77]

God has entrusted us with a powerful gospel. We need to be careful how we present it. Some, for various reasons, have weakened its message. A. W. Tozer in his book *Man, A Dwelling Place for God,* admonishes all who are tempted to water down the gospel:

> The new cross that's being spoken of today does not slay the sinner. It redirects him. It gears him into a cleaner and a jollier way of living and saves his self-respect. To the self-assertive it says, "Come and assert yourself for Christ." To the egotist it says, "Come and do your boasting in the Lord." To the thrill seeker it says, "Come and enjoy the thrill of Christian fellowship." The Christian message is slanted in the direction of the current vogue in order to make it acceptable to the public . . . The faith of Christ does not parallel the world, it intersects it. In coming to Christ, we do not bring our old life onto a higher plain. We leave it at the cross. The corn of wheat must go into the ground and die. We who preach the gospel must not think of ourselves as public relation agents trying to establish good will between God and the world. We must not imagine ourselves commissioned to make Christ acceptable to big business, the press, the world of sports or even modern education. We are not diplomats but prophets, and our message is not a compromise but an ultimatum.[78]

In Romans 1:16, Paul declared that he was not ashamed of the gospel because it is the *"power of God for salvation to everyone who believes."* The Greek word he used there for *power* is the word from which we get the word *dynamite*.

The gospel is explosively powerful! When you dilute it, you strip it of its power to bring people to genuine repentance and change their lives. Share the gospel as graciously, lovingly, and tactfully as possible, but always share it boldly, accurately, and fully. A watered-down gospel is a false gospel.

Point to Ponder

In your own words, explain the essence of the gospel. What are the four elements that should be included?

Defending Your Faith

In addition to communicating the gospel, every Christian should be able to share his or her testimony in five minutes—on the spot. Your testimony is simply your story of what Christ has done for you. Paul shared his salvation testimony with King Agrippa in Acts 26. Peter spoke of *"always [being] prepared to make a defense to anyone who asks you for a reason for the hope that is in you"* (1 Pet. 3:15).

An effective testimony consists of three distinct parts:

1. This is what my life was like before I came to Christ.
2. This is what happened that changed my life (how I came to Christ).
3. This is my life after God saved me.

A testimony is easy to produce, but it is a very powerful tool in sharing Christ with others. A changed life is a living display of the gospel. An anonymous poet once wrote:

> You're writing a gospel, a chapter each day,
>
> By the deeds that you do, and the words that you say.
>
> Men read what you write, whether faithless or true,
>
> Say, what is the gospel, according to you?[79]

Point to Ponder

You should be able to share your testimony in three minutes. Determine to share it with someone this week.

Is it Worth It?

The ultimate purpose of evangelism is the glory of God. Nothing proclaims God's glory any greater than His love for sinful humans, a love so great that He gave His Son to redeem us. The Bible is saturated with passages about the manifestation of God's glory through His redemptive relationship with people. Here are two:

> *The people whom I formed for Myself that they might declare My praise.* (Isa. 43:21)

> *But you are a chosen race, a royal priesthood, a holy nation, a people for His own possession, that you may proclaim the excellencies of Him*

who called you out of darkness into His marvelous light. (1 Pet. 2:9)

Please understand, the *focus* of our evangelism is not the lost. It is God and His glory. The *object* of our evangelism is the lost. We tell others about Jesus because He is worthy of all of their worship. Anglican pastor, commentator, and noted leader of the worldwide evangelical movement, John Stott, summarizes, "Our supreme motivation in world evangelization will not primarily be obedience to the great commission, nor even loving concern for those who do not yet know Jesus, important as these two incentives are, but first and foremost a burning zeal (even 'jealousy') for the glory of Jesus Christ. For God has exalted him to the highest place, and desires everybody to honor him too."[80]

If you say you love God and you love the glory of God, then why are you not talking about Him everywhere you go? If you say you're passionate about God and you're thankful for what He has done for you, why are you not sharing that with people? Do your coworkers know about your relationship with the Lord? Do your family members know about your relationship with Jesus? Do your neighbors know that you love Him? Sharing the good news with people you meet should be a natural expression of your love for Him. Who in your life needs you to show and tell the gospel to them? Are you fostering new friendships? Are you frequenting the same place at the same time to build relationships with the same people? You should be.

If you are a disciple, you will be.

Walking Point

List three friends, family members, or acquaintances who are unsaved. Commit to praying for God to open their hearts to hear the gospel. Then commit to sharing it with them.

Memory Verse
1 Thessalonians 2:8

Chapter 10

C.L.O.S.E.R.

RENEW: H.E.A.R.ING FROM GOD

> *"All Scripture is breathed out by God and profitable for teaching, for reproof, for correction, and for training in righteousness, that the man of God may be complete, equipped for every good work."*
> **2 Timothy 3:16–17**

> "More than almost any other discipline, journaling has a fascinating appeal. . . . One reason is the way journaling blends biblical doctrine and daily living, like the confluence of two great rivers, into one. . . . Although the practice of journaling is not commanded in Scripture, it is modeled. And God has blessed the use of journals since Bible times."
> ***Donald Whitney***

In order to produce lean muscle mass, bodybuilders are trained to eat six protein-filled meals every day. This causes the body's metabolism to work overtime, burning fat more quickly and building muscle. In my quest to be the next professional athlete (before I came to

Christ), I consumed a regular diet of eggs, tuna, eggs, chicken, eggs, turkey, and eggs. The last thing I dared put in my mouth was a candy bar. Why? Because what I put into my body was going to reveal itself on the outside.

Why Should I Read the Bible?

We all know that a healthy diet is the primary key to physical strength and fitness, and the same is true in our spiritual lives. The Bible is to the spirit what food is to the body. If we do not regularly, daily, take God's Word into our minds, hearts, and spirits, we will starve spiritually. Nutritionists tell us that we need to eat three balanced meals every day. Why would any less be true for our spiritual well-being? Many church members are malnourished believers who rarely, if ever, read God's Word other than on Sunday at church. Imagine eating only one meal a week! This, in effect, is the condition of those who only receive something from the Bible at church on Sunday morning.

What does this have to do with discipleship? Discipleship is the process of being conformed to the image of Christ through obedience to the will of God. A heart that obeys God is a heart that has first come to love Him. Our love for God grows as we know Him. The better we know God, the more we love Him. How do we know God? The primary way God has revealed Himself to us is through His Word. A heart that knows God is a heart that has been transformed by the renewing of the mind through the study and application of God's Word. Here, then, is the core of discipleship:

Study the Bible ➡ **Know God** ➡ **Obey God**

Figure 4

An episode out of Jesus's life demonstrates why we need to take God's Word into our hearts daily. Immediately after His baptism, Jesus was subjected to a grueling temptation, the fiercest temptation ever experienced by any man. The Scripture records three temptations hurled by Satan at God's Son. Note the first:

> *Then Jesus was led up by the Spirit into the wilderness to be tempted by the devil. And after fasting forty days and forty nights, he was hungry. And the tempter came and said to him, "If you are the Son of God, command these stones to become loaves of bread." But he answered, "It is written, 'Man shall not live by bread alone, but by every word that comes from the mouth of God.'"* (Matt. 4:1–4)

In each of the three temptations, Jesus resisted Satan by smiting him with the sword of the Spirit, which is the Word of God (Eph. 6:17). Here is the specific verse quoted by Jesus in Matthew 4:4:

> *And he humbled you and let you hunger and fed you with manna, which you did not know, nor did your fathers know, that he might make you know that man does not live by bread alone, but man lives by every word that comes from the mouth of the LORD.* (Deut. 8:3)

Here is the story behind the verse. The book of Exodus records the life of Moses, whom God chose to lead the Israelites out of bondage to Pharaoh and into the flourishing land that He had promised them. Through a series of demonstrations of God's sovereign power, the Israelites left Egypt and fled to the desert.

Without food or water, they were forced to rely solely on God for their daily sustenance. After the people complained to Moses about the absence of food, God revealed how He would provide the food they desperately needed to survive:

> Then the LORD said to Moses, "Behold, I am about to rain bread from heaven for you, and the people shall go out and gather a day's portion every day, that I may test them, whether they will walk in my law or not. On the sixth day, when they prepare what they bring in, it will be twice as much as they gather daily." (Exod. 16:4–5)

The very next day, God did exactly what He had promised: He supplied food for the people in the form of manna (bread). When they first saw the flaky substance on the ground, the people asked if this was the bread that God had promised. Moses answered,

> It is the bread that the LORD has given you to eat. This is what the LORD has commanded: "Gather of it, each one of you, as much as he can eat. You shall each take an omer [2 liters], according to the number of the persons that each of you has in his tent." And the people of Israel did so. They gathered, some more, some less. But when they measured it with an omer, whoever gathered much had nothing left over, and whoever gathered little had no lack. Each of them gathered as much as he could eat. And Moses said to them, "Let no one leave any of it over till the morning." But they did not listen to Moses. Some left part of it till the morning, and it bred worms and stank. (Exod. 16:15–20)

Questions to Consider

*Do you view the Word as
spiritual nourishment for your
soul? If so, in what ways?*

Food for the Soul

The previous passage pinpoints two vital principles for us to apply to our lives. First, the people were
required to gather their own bread each day. Each individual had to personally make time to gather food, and
then put forth the energy and effort to actually collect
it. Second, the bread they gathered was only good for
that particular day. Manna had a short shelf life—less
than twenty-four hours! Every day, with the exception
of the Sabbath, they had to repeat the process of gathering manna.

Every Jew knew the story of the manna. In His hour
of temptation, Jesus connected the manna (bread) with
the Word of God. Look at some key points of Jesus's
lesson to us:

- As spiritual beings, we need more than physical nourishment (bread) to survive
- Our spiritual nourishment (spiritual bread) is
  the Word of God
- God's Word is to us what the manna was to
  the ancient Jews: life-sustaining nourishment
- Just as the Jews had to make the time and
  effort to gather manna, we must set aside time
  every day to be spiritually nourished from the
  Bible

- Just as the Jews had to gather manna daily, we must read the Bible *every* day. What we read today is not sufficient for tomorrow.

In addition to bread, the Lord compares His Word to milk (1 Pet. 2:2), meat (1 Cor. 3:2; Heb. 5:12–14), and honey (Ps. 119:103; Ezra 3:1–3). The Bible supplies the complete spiritual nourishment we need: bread, milk, and meat. It is not something we must force down for our own good. It is sweet, like honey, and delightful to the taste.

From the beginning of Genesis through the end of Revelation, God's Word has always accomplished what He intended it to accomplish (Is. 55:11). Hebrews 1:13 says, *"God sustains all things by the Word of truth."* Then Hebrews 4:12 reveals, *"The Word of God is living and active and sharper than any two-edged sword, piercing even to the division of soul and spirit, discerning the thoughts and intentions of our own hearts."* James 1:18 teaches that God chose to give us birth through the Word of truth. The Word does the work in our lives.

Point to Ponder

Describe your pattern for reading the Bible over the past weeks or months.

Confessions of a Bored Bible Reader

People create a multitude of excuses as to why they do not read the Bible. While I was finishing my seminary degree, I flew back and forth every week for class. On every trip I asked the person sitting next to me on the plane some variation of the same question: "Why do you believe people are not reading the Bible? Or, for that matter, why aren't *you* reading the Bible?" The most common responses were: "I don't have enough time." "It doesn't have any bearing on my life." "I don't know what it means." "The Bible is confusing to me." "It is too old." "I have read it before and didn't get anything out of it." The most revealing excuse I heard was, "The Bible doesn't speak to me."

Polling the passengers on the plane caused me to question my own quiet time. After an honest examination, I realized that my own quiet time bordered on being routine and mundane. In an attempt to add fresh life to studying God's Word, I tried a number of different Bible reading plans. I began reading one Old Testament passage, one New Testament passage, and one Psalm every day. Before long, however, I found myself more interested in checking off boxes on my Bible reading calendar than hearing from God.

One year, I attempted to follow a plan of reading through the books of Scripture consecutively. This worked for a while, but when I came to Leviticus, I had trouble concentrating on the reading. Instead, I found myself dozing off, or thinking about an upcoming appointment or a meeting from the previous day.

Another plan was to read the Old Testament once and the New Testament twice during the course of a year. For the most part, every plan accomplished its purpose, which was to read through the Bible in a year. But with each plan, I never experienced spiritual fulfillment. I never saw God's true purpose for Bible reading accomplished in my life.

After much prayer, I realized that the problem was not with the reading plan, but with the reader following the plan. When I was brutally honest with the man in the mirror, I acknowledged that I was not listening for a word from God, nor was I looking for ways to apply God's truth to my life. What I needed was something that would help create an atmosphere where I could hear from God.

A Time to be Quiet

If you are going to be a disciple of Christ, you *must* have a daily quiet time with God. It is absolutely irreplaceable for your spiritual development. You must make it a priority in your life, setting aside time in your daily schedule for God to speak to you.

Many suggest rising early in the morning to spend time in God's Word. An overwhelming number of Scripture passages recommend this discipline. A number of the Psalms, for example, speak of waking up early in the morning to communicate with God (see Pss. 5 and 88). Jesus Himself rose before daylight for intimate communion with His Father (Mark 1:35). I know many, many believers who follow this practice from the conviction that we need to begin our days, before facing anything or anyone else, by seeking the Lord and receiving strength and wisdom from His Word. Two men whom I once mentored spent every morning before work in their vehicles, alone with God.

Personally, my private time with the Lord is at night, shortly before going to bed. It is a precious time when I replay the events of the day, take captive every thought, and focus on the Lord.

The point is simple: you must select a time of day that works best for you, and set it apart for the Lord. Choose a place where you can be alone with Him and His Word, a quiet place where you can listen to Him. If you will focus your full attention on His Word, He will speak to you through His Spirit, who lives within you. If the atmosphere is noisy or congested, then you will have a difficult time hearing from God.

God has extended to you, His child, an open invitation into His presence (Heb. 4:16). Think of it: God invites you to approach Him whenever you would like. His door is always open to you. He tells you not to be nervous or fearful, and not to be concerned with disturbing Him. Instead, He beckons you to approach His throne with boldness and confidence.

Why would you not accept this gracious invitation, issued personally to you from the Creator of the universe, who now just happens to call Himself your Father, because of your relationship with His Son, Jesus Christ?

If You Fail to Plan, then Plan to Fail

Antoine de Saint-Exupery, the French poet and author of *The Little Prince,* hit the nail on the head when he said, "A goal without a plan is just a wish."[81] Nothing could be truer when it comes to our devotional lives and studying God's Word. In order to grow in your devotional life, you must have a plan.

When I was a new believer, I used the "OPRA" technique for reading the Bible: I would randomly OPEN the Bible, POINT to a passage, READ the verse, and try to figure out a way to APPLY it to my life. Thankfully, I didn't land on the Scripture that says, *"He [speaking of Judas Iscariot] went and hanged himself"* (Matt. 27:5).

Reading random Scriptures will not provide solid biblical growth any more than eating random foods out of your pantry will provide solid physical growth. An effective reading plan is required. While there are many plans out there, it is important to find one that works for you, and stick to it (Appendix 4 contains a sample Bible reading plan).

What is a good starting point for reading Scripture? I have often encouraged my discipleship groups to begin by reading 2 Timothy every day. The Apostle

Paul wrote to Timothy, whom he discipled, about many of the most important truths for the Christian life. Only four chapters long, 2 Timothy can be easily read in its entirety every day. After a week, you will have read through the entire book seven times. By doing so, you will be able to move beyond mere casual reading to uncovering the applicable truths of the book. Words that you might quickly pass over in casual reading will come alive with each additional reading. Another good way to begin your journey in God's Word is by reading 1 John every day. Like 2 Timothy, it discusses many of the basic truths of the Christian life in a few short chapters.

Many new believers ask how much time they should spend in God's Word each day. At certain times of the day, our quiet time might be limited by other priorities. This is especially true in the morning, as most of us have to work for a living! Generally speaking, however, we should not put parameters on God. I have spent as short as five minutes alone with the Lord, and as long as a few hours poring over the Scriptures. Because God is not bound by time, we should not put a time restraint on Him.

Remember that what you put into something determines what you get out of it. This is true in your devotional life. A quiet time is for more than just reading God's Word. It also includes waiting on God to speak and listening to Him. We cannot force God to speak or act within our schedules. The Lord speaks and works according to His perfect timing. He is not in a rush, and you shouldn't be either. While it is not always possible, plan some open-ended times into your schedule to spend with the Lord.

Question to Consider

*Why is having a Bible reading
plan important?*

Choose Your Sword

We live in a time when many translations of the
Bible are available. Many believers question which version is best, and which one they should use. Basically,
translation teams take one of two approaches when
converting the Hebrew (Old Testament) and Greek
(New Testament) texts to English. Some translate
the Scripture strictly word-for-word from the original
texts. Simply put, others translate a thought or concept, rather than individual words. In theological circles, the process of literal, word-for-word translation is
called *formal equivalence.* Formal equivalence also pre-
serves the grammar of the preserved Scripture texts.
The other approach, expressing an entire thought or
concept, is referred to as *dynamic equivalence.*

A third category is the *paraphrase.* Essentially, a
paraphrase is a version in which the translator (or author)
expresses the Scripture in his own words. *The Message* and
the *Living Bible* are popular paraphrases. Paraphrases
can be helpful or inspirational, but it is best to read them
alongside an actual translation of God's Word.

Many people prefer dynamic equivalents, such as
the *New International Version* (NIV) or *New Living
Translation* (NLT), because they feel they are easier
to read and understand. However, these versions
are more subjective than word-for-word translations,
because they require the translators to inject their own

understanding of Scripture into the text. This is not to say that these versions are untrustworthy, nor is it to say that they should be avoided.

I recommend that you choose a translation closer to the original languages as your primary version for Bible reading and study. God has not only imparted His divine, eternal truth to us in the statements of the Bible, but also in the words themselves. In studying God's Word, your desire will be to know the exact word used in the particular passage you are reading. For this reason, word-for-word translations such as the *English Standard Version* (ESV), the *Holman Christian Standard Bible* (HCSB, which actually employs both formal and dynamic equivalence), the *New American Standard Bible* (NASB), the *King James Version* (KJV), and the *New King James Version* (NKJV) are preferable.

Ultimately, the best translation is the one that gets read. Many who argue for a particular translation over another may never read the one they are proposing. Overall, the translation that you will faithfully read and study is the best translation for you.

Creating an Atmosphere to H.E.A.R. from God

The H.E.A.R. journaling method promotes reading the Bible with a life-transforming purpose. No longer will your focus be on checking off the boxes on your daily reading schedule; your purpose will instead be to read in order to understand and respond to God's Word.

The acronym H.E.A.R. stands for **HIGHLIGHT, EXPLAIN, APPLY**, and **RESPOND**.[82] Each of these four steps contributes to creating an atmosphere to hear God speak. After settling on a reading plan and establishing a time for studying God's Word, you will be ready to H.E.A.R. from God.

Let's assume that you begin your quiet time with the book of 2 Timothy, and today's reading is the first chapter of the book. Before reading the text, pause to sincerely ask God to speak to you. It may seem trite, but it is absolutely imperative that we seek God's guidance in order to understand His Word. Remember, we need the help of the Holy Spirit to understand the truths that God has revealed to us in His Word (1 Cor. 2:12–14). Every time we open our Bibles, we should pray the simple prayer that David prayed: *"Open my eyes, that I may behold wondrous things out of your law (Word)"* (Ps. 119:18).

After praying for the Holy Spirit's guidance, open your notebook or journal, and at the top left-hand corner, write the letter H. (Appendix 3 contains examples of completed H.E.A.R. entries.) This exercise will remind you to read with a purpose. In the course of your reading, one or two verses will usually stand out and speak to you. After reading the passage of Scripture, **HIGHLIGHT** each verse that speaks to you by copying it under the letter "H". Write out the following:

> **The name of the book**
>
> **The passage of Scripture**
>
> **The chapter and verse numbers that especially speak to you**
>
> **A title to describe the passage**

This practice will make it easier to find the passage when you want to revisit it in the future.

After you have highlighted the passage, write the letter "E" under the previous entry. At this stage you will **EXPLAIN** what the text means. By asking some simple questions, with the help of God's Spirit, you can understand the meaning of a passage or verse. The next chapter will teach you in detail how to understand the meaning of a passage. Until then, here are a few questions to get you started:

Why was this written?

To whom was it originally written?

How does it fit with the verses before and after it?

Why did the Holy Spirit include this passage in the book?

What is He intending to communicate through this text?

At this point, you are beginning the process of discovering the specific and personal word that God has for you from His Word. What is important is that you are engaging the text and wrestling with its meaning.

After writing a short summary of what you think the text means, write the letter "A" below the letter "E". Under the "A", write the word **APPLY**. This application is the heart of the process. Everything culminates under this heading. As you have done before, ask a series of questions to uncover the significance of these verses to you personally, questions like:

How can this help me?

What does this mean today?

What would the application of this verse look like in my life?

What does this mean to me?

What is God saying to me?

These questions bridge the gap between the ancient world and your world today. They provide a way for God to speak to you from the specific passage or verse. Answer these questions under the "A". Challenge yourself to write between two and five sentences about how the text applies to your life.

Finally, below the first three entries, write the letter "R" for **RESPOND**. Your response to the passage may take on many forms. You may write a call to action. You may describe how you will be different because of what God has said to you through His Word. You may indicate what you are going to do because of what you have learned. You may respond by writing out a prayer to God. For example, you may ask God to help you to be more loving, or to give you a desire to be more generous in your giving. Keep in mind that this is your response to what you have just read.

Notice that all of the words in the H.E.A.R. formula are action words: **HIGHLIGHT**, **EXPLAIN**, **APPLY**, and **RESPOND**. God does not want us to sit back and wait for Him to drop some truth into our laps. Instead of waiting passively, God desires that we actively pursue Him. Jesus said,

> *Ask, and it will be given to you; seek, and you will find; knock, and it will be opened to you.* (Matt. 7:7)

Think of the miracle of the Bible. Over centuries of time, God supernaturally moved upon a number of men in an unusual way that resulted in them writing the exact words of God. God led His people to recognize these divine writings, and to distinguish them from everything else that has ever been written. Then God's people brought these sixty-six books together. The preservation and survival of the Bible is as miraculous as its writing. Then God gave men, beginning with Gutenberg's printing press, technological knowledge to copy and transmit the Bible so that all people could have it. All because God has something to say to *you.*

Yet many professing Christians never open the Bible, other than on Sunday. We will surely answer to God one day for what we did or did not do with His Word.

Evangelist Robert L. Sumner in his book *The Wonder of the Word of God* relates the challenging story of a man in Kansas City, who was badly injured in an explosion. After losing his eyesight and the use of both hands, the man was greatly distraught, for he could never read the Bible again. His distress turned into joy after hearing of a woman in England who read Braille with her lips. He searched and found a copy of the Bible in Braille. Sadly, he was discouraged again when he realized the nerve endings in his lips were too damaged to recognize the characters on the pages. One day, as he lifted the raised lettering up to his lips, his tongue touched a few of the letters. He thought to himself, "I could read the Bible with my tongue."[83]

At the time of writing, Robert Sumner reported that the man had read through the entire Bible four times with his tongue. Prayerfully, this man will not be standing next to you (or me) when we are called before the Bema Seat of Christ. His diligence is a convicting reminder that there will be no excuse for laziness in regard to reading or memorizing God's Word.

Walking Point

*Commit to logging a H.E.A.R.
entry for the next five days.*

H. E. A. R. journal suggestions for the week:
Read Psalm 119:1-18. Focus on verses 10–11.
Read 2 Timothy 3:1-17. Focus on verses 16–17.
Read James 1:1-27. Focus on verses. 22-24.
Read 1 John 5. Focus on verse. 3.
Read 2 Peter 1. Focus on verse 21.

Memory Verse
John 1:1–2

Afterword

WHERE DO WE GO FROM HERE?

I am your constant companion. I am your greatest helper or heaviest burden. I will push you onward or drag you down to failure. I am completely at your command. Half the things you do you might just as well turn over to me, and I will be able to do them quickly and correctly. I am easily managed—you must merely be firm with me. Show me exactly how you want something done and after a few lessons, I will do it automatically. I am the servant of all great men; and alas, of all failures, as well. Those who are great, I have made great. Those who are failures, I have made failures. I am not a machine, though I work with all the precision of a machine plus the intelligence of a man. You may run me for profit or run me for ruin—it makes no difference to me. Take me, train me, be firm with me, and I will place the world at your feet. Be easy with me and I will destroy you. Who am I? I am Habit.[84]

Have you ever stopped to consider how much of your life is determined by habits? Almost everything we do is the result of our habits. The way we talk, walk, drive, eat, bathe, and interact with others is the direct product of the habits we develop.

Habits will either be stumbling blocks that hinder us or stepping stones that help us in the spiritual growth process. Godly habits cultivate a life of obedience, especially in a discipleship group. As with any spiritual discipline, practice moves us from duty to devotion, and ultimately, delight.

The Sticking Point

How long does a person have to maintain a discipline before it becomes a habit? After studying patients at different intervals from 18 to 254 days, scientists at the University College of London determined that it takes sixty-six days for a practice to become a habit.

Many people give up long before this. Think about how many days you went to the gym in January before falling off the wagon. Think about how long you stuck with that new diet. Now you know why those pounds stuck to you. If you are like most people, you have given up on some positive practice before it could become a habit.

If you have used this book as a manual for your discipleship group, over the past ten weeks you have disciplined yourself by journaling H.E.A.R. entries, memorizing Scripture, praying, obeying God, and sharing the gospel with others.

That is long enough for each of these practices to become godly habits in your life. Now, it's up to you to continue practicing what you have learned through this book in your D-Group. Continue meeting weekly to quote Scripture aloud, pray together, and ask each other probing questions about life, marriage, ministry, and profession. Make your H.E.A.R. entries the center-piece of your weekly discussion, spending time sharing what God said to each of you from the Word and how you all applied it to your lives.

Another option for your D-Group is to read a selected book that addresses a particular need in your lives. If group members are struggling in their mar-riages, read a book on strengthening your relationship with your spouse. If someone in the group is dealing with sin, study a book addressing idols of the heart. Most of my groups have worked through theology books such as Wayne Grudem's *Bible Doctrines* book or his smaller resource *Christian Beliefs: Twenty Basics Every Christian Should Know.* New or growing believ-ers would benefit from walking through books such as *Choose the Life* by Bill Hull, *Discipleship Essentials* by Greg Ogden, or *What the Bible Says to the Believer: The Believer's Personal Handbook.*[85] (A list of resources can be found in Appendix 10.) Whatever resources you choose, remember that the material serves as a plat-form for meeting and growing with other believers.

Essential Reading

As I have already mentioned, daily Bible reading is essential for spiritual growth. While there are many Bible reading plans to choose from, I want to recommend the F-260.

This is a reading plan designed to take you through the whole Bible in a year, but it is divided into easily digestible daily readings. It is called the F-260 because, in 260 days, you will read every foundational passage of Scripture. You can download this reading plan for free at replicate.org or see it in Appendix 4. You can also check out the resources we've put together at replicate.org/dgroup.

At this point, I am certain you have more questions than answers. Appendix 9 addresses common questions that arise in the disciple-making process.

Don't Fumble the Handoff

Established in 1958, the Queen's Baton Relay initiates the Commonwealth Games. Similar to the passing of the Olympic torch, the Queen's baton is handed to a runner to begin the relay race. Unlike the torch, however, this baton has a handwritten note tucked inside. The race traditionally begins at Buckingham Palace in London, and the baton travels through nations competing in the Games. In the Opening Ceremony of the Games, the final runner hands the baton back to the Queen, who removes the note from the baton and reads it aloud to the people. In the 2006 Games, held in Melbourne, Australia, the baton was carried 112,000 miles through all seventy-one nations of the Commonwealth. After a year and a day, the baton was returned to the Queen. That's a pretty impressive relay race, right?

We're running a relay race, too. The author of Hebrews stated, *"Therefore, since we are surrounded by so great a cloud of witnesses, let us also lay aside every weight, and sin which clings so closely, and let us run with endurance the race that is set before us, looking to Jesus, the founder and perfecter of our faith"* (Heb. 12:1–2). Jesus passed the baton to His followers almost 2,000 years ago, by saying, *"Go therefore and make disciples of all nations, baptizing them in the name of the Father and of the Son and of the Holy Spirit, teaching them to observe all that I have commanded you"* (Matt. 28:19–20).

Before ascending to heaven, Jesus passed the baton to His disciples, His loyal followers. Peter received the handoff from Jesus. Although he denied Jesus three times in the courtyard, Jesus restored him on the Sea of Galilee, asking him the same question three times— *"Peter, do you love Me?"*—before describing the way he would die (John 21:15–19). Tradition says that Peter was crucified upside down because he did not feel worthy to die in the same manner as his Lord. As the nails pierced Peter's wrists, the baton fell into the hands of a man named Ignatius.

In AD 107, a judge threatened to throw Ignatius to the lions if he did not recant his faith in Christ. Ignatius boldly resisted the request of the judge with these words: "I am the wheat of Christ, ground by the teeth of beasts to become pure bread." His fate was sealed. As soon as his body was cast onto the floor of that den, the lions forcibly shredded his flesh into pieces. But before he died, the baton fell again, this time into the hands of a man named Polycarp.

Polycarp, Greek Bishop of Smyrna, was arrested during a pagan festival for refusing to burn incense to the emperor. Under pressure to recant his faith in Christ or face death, the old man refused, exclaiming, "For eighty-six years, I have served Him. How then can I blaspheme my King and Savior? Bring forth what thou will." Subsequently, his hands and feet were fastened to a stake, where he was torched for his faith in Christ. As the flames climbed his legs, the baton fell into the hands of a man named William Tyndale.

We are indebted to Tyndale for the Bible we read today. In 1526, he was the first to translate the original Greek and Hebrew manuscripts into English. Much of Tyndale's work found its way into the *King James Version* less than a century later. Instead of receiving praise for his diligent efforts, he was welcomed with persecution. Tyndale was arrested in 1535 and jailed in the castle of Vilvoorde outside Brussels for over a year. Later, he was tried for heresy and burned at the stake. As he breathed his last, Tyndale passed the baton to new generations of runners.

Some of the subsequent carriers of the baton have stories of struggles and failures, but more tales abound of restoration and triumph. Recent pages of history continue the saga of those who have been handed the baton and have faithfully carried the message of Jesus Christ. The intent is clear: Jesus wants His baton to be carried and passed along.

Hold your hands out in front of you with your palms up. Really, do it. See what is in your hands. Whether or not you feel worthy or ready, the baton has been passed to you. What will you do with it? Will you fumble the handoff, or will you run with passion and conviction? Will you make disciples? Just as the Queen gave a baton to her messengers to take around the country, the King of Kings has given us a baton to take to the world. One day we will meet the King of the Universe face to face and give an account of how well we carried the baton. What if Jesus's last words to His disciples are His first words to you and me? What if the message in the baton reads, "Well done, good and faithful servant!"? Do not be deceived. He will not say "Well done," if you have not done well.

Take the baton, run the race, and pass it on.

Eternity is at stake.

Will Allen Dromgoole captured the essence of discipleship in the poem, *Bridge Builders*:

> *An old man, going a lone highway,*
> *Came at evening, cold and gray;*
> *To a chasm, vast and deep and wide,*
> *Through which was flowing a sullen tide.*
> *The old man crossed the twilight dim—*
> *That sullen stream had no fears for him;*
> *But he turned, when he had reached the other side,*
> *He built a bridge to span the tide.*

"Old man," said a fellow pilgrim near,
"You are wasting strength building here,
Your journey will end with the ending day;
You never again will pass this way.
You have crossed the chasm, deep and wide,
Why build up the bridge at the eventide?"

The builder lifted his old gray head.
"Good friend, in the path I have come," he said.
"There follows after me today
A youth whose feet must pass this way.
The chasm that has been naught to me
To that fair-haired youth may a pitfall be.
He, too, must cross in the twilight dim;
Good friend, I am building the bridge for him."[86]

Question to Consider

I believe that when we stand before the Lord Jesus Christ, He will ask us this question: Whom have you discipled?

What will your answer be?

DISCIPLE-MAKING COVENANT

I will commit to the following expectations:

1. I pledge myself fully to the Lord with the anticipation that I am entering a time of accelerated spiritual transformation.

2. I will meet with my D-Group for approximately one and one-half hours every week, unless providentially hindered.

3. I will complete all assignments on a weekly basis before my D-Group meeting, in order to contribute to the discussion.

4. I will contribute to an atmosphere of confidentiality, honesty, and transparency for the edification of others in the group as well as my own spiritual growth.

5. I will pray every week for the other men/women who are on the discipleship journey with me.

6. I will begin praying about replicating the discipleship process upon completion of this group.

Signed Mentee _____

Signed Mentor _____

Date _____

Appendix 2

SPIRITUAL JOURNEY INVENTORY

Use these questions in your D-Group to get acquainted with each other.

1. After coming to the Lord, I finally understood _____.

2. The closest I have felt to God in my life was _____.

3. The farthest I felt from God was _____.

4. If I could change one incident in my life it would be _____. Why?

5. One incident in my life that I would never change would be _____. Why?

6. The turning point in my relationship with God was _____. Why?

Appendix 3

SAMPLE H.E.A.R. ENTRY

Read: Philippians 4:10–13   **Date:** 11–30–13   **Title:** Secret of Contentment

H (Highlight) *"I can do all things through Christ who strengthens me."* (Phil. 4:13)

E (Explain) Paul was telling the church at Philippi that he has discovered the secret of contentment. No matter the situation in Paul's life, he realized that Christ was all he needed, and Christ was the one who strengthened him to persevere through difficult times.

A (Apply) In my life, I will experience many ups and downs. My contentment is not found in circumstances. Rather, it is based on my relationship with Jesus Christ. Only Jesus gives me the strength I need to be content in every circumstance of life.

R (Respond) Lord Jesus, please help me as I strive to be content in You. Through Your strength, I can make it through any situation I must face.

Appendix 4

SAMPLE BIBLE READING PLAN

Week 1
Genesis 1–2
Genesis 3–4
Genesis 6–7
Genesis 8–9
Job 1–2
Memory Verses:
Genesis 1:27
Hebrews 11:7

Week 2
Job 38–39
Job 40–42
Genesis 11–12
Genesis 15
Genesis 16–17
Memory Verses:
Hebrews 11:6
Hebrews 11:8–10

Week 3
Genesis 18–19
Genesis 20–21
Genesis 22

Genesis 24
Genesis 25:19–34,
26
Memory Verses:
Romans 4:20–22
Hebrews 11:17–19

Week 4
Genesis 27–28
Genesis 29–30:24
Genesis 31–32
Genesis 33, 35
Genesis 37
Memory Verses:
2 Corinthians
10:12
1 John 3:18

Week 5
Genesis 39–40
Genesis 41
Genesis 42–43
Genesis 44–45
Genesis 46–47

Memory Verses:
Romans 8:28–30
Ephesians 3:20–21

Week 6
Genesis 48–49
Genesis 50–Exodus
1
Exodus 2–3
Exodus 4–5
Exodus 6–7
Memory Verses:
Genesis 50:20
Hebrews 11:24–26

Week 7
Exodus 8–9
Exodus 10–11
Exodus 12
Exodus 13:17–14
Exodus 16–17
Memory Verses:
John 1:29
Hebrews 9:22

Week 8
Exodus 19–20
Exodus 24–25
Exodus 26–27
Exodus 28–29
Exodus 30–31
Memory Verses:
Exodus 20:1–3
Galatians 5:14

Week 9
Exodus 32–33
Exodus 34–36:1
Exodus 40
Leviticus 8–9
Leviticus 16–17
Memory Verses:
Exodus 33:16
Matthew 22:37–39

Week 10
Leviticus 23
Leviticus 26
Numbers 11–12
Numbers 13–14
Numbers 16–17
Memory Verses:
Leviticus 26:13
Deuteronomy
31:7–8

Week 11
Numbers 20,
27:12–23
Numbers 34–35
Deuteronomy 1–2
Deuteronomy 3–4
Deuteronomy 6–7
Memory Verses:

Deuteronomy 4:7
Deuteronomy
6:4–9

Week 12
Deuteronomy 8–9
Deuteronomy
30–31
Deuteronomy
32:48–52, 34
Joshua 1–2
Joshua 3–4
Memory Verses:
Joshua 1:8–9
Psalm 1:1–2

Week 13
Joshua 5:10–15, 6
Joshua 7–8
Joshua 23–24
Judges 2–3
Judges 4
Memory Verses:
Joshua 24:14–15
Judges 2:12

Week 14
Judges 6–7
Judges 13–14
Judges 15–16
Ruth 1–2
Ruth 3–4
Memory Verses:
Psalm 19:14
Galatians 4:4–5

Week 15
1 Samuel 1–2
1 Samuel 3, 8

1 Samuel 9-10
1 Samuel 13–14
1 Samuel 15–16
Memory Verses:
1 Samuel 15:22
1 Samuel 16:7

Week 16
1 Samuel 17–18
1 Samuel 19–20
1 Samuel 21–22
Psalm 22,
1 Samuel 24–25:1
1 Samuel 28; 31
Memory Verses:
1 Samuel 17:46–47
2 Timothy 4:17a

Week 17
2 Samuel 1, 2:1–7
2 Samuel 3:1, 5,
Psalm 23
2 Samuel 6–7
Psalm 18, 2
Samuel 9
2 Samuel 11–12
Memory Verses:
Psalm 23:1–3
Psalm 51:10–13

Week 18
Psalm 51
2 Samuel 24,
Psalm 24
Psalms 1, 19
Psalms 103,
119:1–48
Psalms
119:49–128

Memory Verses:
Psalm 1:1–7
Psalm 119:7–11

Week 19
Psalms 119:129–176, 139
Psalms 148–150
1 Kings 2
1 Kings 3, 6
1 Kings 8, 9:1–9
Memory Verses:
Psalm 139:1–3
Psalm 139:15–16

Week 20
Proverbs 1–2
Proverbs 3–4
Proverbs 16–18
Proverbs 31
1 Kings 11–12
Memory Verses:
Proverbs 1:7
Proverbs 3:5–6

Week 21
1 Kings 16:29–34, 17
1 Kings 18–19
1 Kings 21–22
2 Kings 2
2 Kings 5, 6:1–23
Memory Verses:
Psalm 17:15
Psalm 63:1

WEEK 22
Jonah 1–2
Jonah 3–4

Hosea 1–3
Amos 1:1, 9
Joel 1–3
Memory Verses:
Psalm 16:11
John 11:25–26

Week 23
Isaiah 6, 9
Isaiah 44–45
Isaiah 52–53
Isaiah 65–66
Micah 1, 4:6–13, 5
Memory Verses:
Isaiah 53:5–6
1 Peter 2:23–24

Week 24
2 Kings 17–18
2 Kings 19–21
2 Kings 22–23
Jeremiah 1–3:5
Jeremiah 25, 29
Memory Verses:
Proverbs 29:18
Jeremiah 1:15

Week 25
Jeremiah 31:31–40, 32–33
Jeremiah 52,
2 Kings 24–25
Ezekiel 1:1–3, 36:16–38, 37
Daniel 1–2
Daniel 3–4
Memory Verses:
Ezekiel 36:26–27
Daniel 4:35

Week 26
Daniel 5–6
Daniel 9–10, 12
Ezra 1–2
Ezra 3–4
Ezra 5–6
Memory Verses:
Daniel 6:26–27
Daniel 9:19

Week 27
Zechariah 1:1–6, 2, 12
Ezra 7–8
Ezra 9–10
Esther 1–2
Esther 3–4
Memory Verses:
Zephaniah 3:17
1 Peter 3:15

Week 28
Esther 5–7
Esther 8–10
Nehemiah 1–2
Nehemiah 3–4
Nehemiah 5–6
Memory Verses:
Deuteronomy 29:29
Psalm 101:3–4

Week 29
Nehemiah 7–8
Nehemiah 9
Nehemiah 10
Nehemiah 11
Nehemiah 12
Memory Verses:

Nehemiah 6:9
Nehemiah 9:6

Week 30
Nehemiah 13
Malachi 1
Malachi 2
Malachi 3
Malachi 4
Memory Verses:
Psalm 51:17
Colossians 1:19–20

Week 31
Luke 1
Luke 2
Matthew 1–2
Mark 1
John 1
Memory Verses:
John 1:1–2
John 1:14

Week 32
Matthew 3–4
Matthew 5
Matthew 6
Matthew 7
Matthew 8
Memory Verses:
Matthew 5:16
Matthew 6:33

Week 33
Luke 9:10–62
Mark 9-10
Luke 12
John 3–4
Luke 14

Memory Verses:
Luke 14:26–27
Luke 14:33

Week 34
John 6
Matthew 19:16–30
Luke 15—
Luke 17:11–37, 18
Mark 10
Memory Verses:
Mark 10:45
John 6:37

Week 35
John 11, Matthew
21:1–13
John 13
John 14–15
John 16
Matthew 24:1–31
Memory Verse:
John 13:34–35
John 15:4–5

Week 36
Matthew 24:32–51
John 17
Matthew
26:35–27:31
Matthew
27:32–66,
Luke 23:26–56
John 19
Memory Verses:
Luke 23:34
John 17:3

Week 37

Mark 16
Luke 24
John 20–21
Matthew 28
Acts 1
Memory Verses:
Matthew 28:18–20
Acts 1:8

Week 38
Acts 2–3
Acts 4–5
Acts 6
Acts 7
Acts 8–9
Memory Verse:
Acts 2:42
Acts 4:31

Week 39
Acts 10–11
Acts 12
Acts 13–14
James 1–2
James 3–5
Memory Verses:
James 1:2–4
James 2:17

Week 40
Acts 15–16
Galatians 1–3
Galatians 4–6
Acts 17–18:17
1 Thessalonians
1–2
Memory Verses:
Acts 17:11
Acts 17:24–25

Week 41
1 Thessalonians
3–5
2 Thessalonians
1–3
Acts 18:18–28, 19
1 Corinthians 1–2
1 Corinthians 3–4
Memory Verses:
1 Corinthians 1:18
1 Thessalonians
5:23–24

Week 42
1 Corinthians 5–6
1 Corinthians 7–8
1 Corinthians
9–10
1 Corinthians
11–12
1 Corinthians
13–14
Memory Verses:
1 Corinthians
10:13
1 Corinthians
13:13

Week 43
1 Corinthians
15-16
2 Corinthians 1–2
2 Corinthians 3–4
2 Corinthians 5–6
2 Corinthians 7–8
Memory Verses:
Romans 1:16–17
1 Corinthians
15:3–4

Week 44
2 Corinthians
9–10
2 Corinthians
11–13
Romans 1–2, Acts
20:1–3
Romans 3–4
Romans 5–6
Memory Verses:
Romans 5:1
2 Corinthians 10:4

Week 45
Romans 7–8
Romans 9–10
Romans 11–12
Romans 13–14
Romans 15–16
Memory Verses:
Romans 8:1
Romans 12:1–2

Week 46
Acts 20–21
Acts 22–23
Acts 24–25
Acts 26–27
Acts 28
Memory Verses:
Acts 20:24
2 Corinthians
4:7–10

Week 47
Colossians 1–2
Colossians 3–4
Ephesians 1–2
Ephesians 3–4

Ephesians 5–6
Memory Verses:
Ephesians 2:8–10
Colossians 2:6–7

Week 48
Philippians 1–2
Philippians 3–4
Hebrews 1–2
Hebrews 3–4
Hebrews 5–6
Memory Verses:
Philippians 3:7–8
Hebrews 4:14–16

Week 49
Hebrews 7
Hebrews 8–9
Hebrews 10
Hebrews 11
Hebrews 12
Memory Verses:
Galatians 2:19–20
2 Corinthians 5:17

Week 50
1 Timothy 1–3
1 Timothy 4–6
2 Timothy 1–2
2 Timothy 3–4
1 Peter 1–2
Memory Verses:
2 Timothy 2:1–2
2 Timothy 2:15

Week 51
1 Peter 3–4
1 Peter 5, 2 Peter
1

2 Peter 2–3
1 John 1–3
1 John 4–5
Memory Verses:
1 Peter 2:11
1 John 4:10–11

Revelation 2–3
Revelation 4–5
Revelation 18–19
Revelation 20–22
Memory Verses:
Revelation 3:19
Revelation 21:3–4

Week 52
Revelation 1

https://replicate.org/f260-bible-reading-plan

Appendix 5

PRAYER LOG

Date Asked	Prayer Request	Date Answered

Appendix 6

SAMPLE SCRIPTURE
MEMORY CARD

You then, my child, be strengthened
by the grace that is in Christ Jesus,
and what you have heard from me
in the presence of many witnesses
entrust to faithful men who will
be able to teach others also.

2 Timothy 2:1-2

Appendix 7

ACCOUNTABILITY QUESTIONS

1. Have you spent time in the Word and in prayer this week?

2. Have you shared the gospel or your testimony with an unbeliever this week?

3. Have you spent quality time with your family this week?

4. Have you viewed anything immoral this week?

5. Have you had any lustful thoughts or tempting attitudes this week?

6. Have you told any lies or half-truths to put yourself in a positive light before others?

7. Have you participated in anything unethical this week?

8. Have you lied about any of your answers today?

Appendix 8

AVENUES FOR BUILDING RELATIONSHIPS

1. Pray

We need to approach each day with focused prayer. When I pray, "Lord, put someone in my path with whom I can share the gospel," the opportunity usually arises. D. James Kennedy said, "Evangelism without prayer is presumption."[87] Needless to say, prayer is necessary.

2. Frequent a Place

By going regularly to the same places for coffee or lunch, you will develop relationships with employees and other regular customers. Introduce yourself, remember others' names, and start greeting folks by using their names. This will absolutely make you stand out from other customers. Using a person's name displays a genuine interest in him as an individual. Regular contact, smiling, and using people's names are easy ways to open the door to sharing the gospel.

3. Take an Unbeliever to Lunch

People are more likely to talk about their lives over lunch than in any other setting. The casual atmosphere and defined time frame enable people to relax and "open up" about their lives. You will be amazed at how many people desire to talk to a friend.

4. Invite the Neighbors for Dinner

Reach out to each couple or family in your neighborhood (one at a time) by inviting them into your home for an informal meal. Intentionally provide a comfortable, relaxing atmosphere. Do not immediately plunge into the subject of church and salvation, but build a relationship by showing them that you genuinely care. Talk about your kids, your yards, the community—things you already have in common. Keep the conversation friendly. This is not the time and place for discussions about social, economic, or political viewpoints. Remember, you're on a mission to show them Christ in your life in order that you can tell them about Him.

5. Join Your Neighborhood Association

We all enjoy talking about our homes and neighborhoods. Joining your association is a great way to meet people with whom you already have something in common.

6. Join a Club or Group

If you are a student, join a club at school. If you own a business, join a trade group. Or find an interest-based group, such as a biking club, running club, bowling league, or health spa. At Brainerd Baptist Church we have a community facility that houses a coffee shop, meeting rooms, exercise equipment, and health classes. We are very excited that approximately 2,700 of the 3,000 members do not go to our church. What an opportunity for relational evangelism!

7. Go Where People Are

Visit community playgrounds, parks, pools, or other open areas often. Go out in public in a casual way. The more you are outside, the more informal conversations you will have with people. Take a walk. Make eye contact with people. Smile and say hello. Be ready with a gentle word to begin conversations on casual, everyday subjects, even the weather. Be interested in what others say. When asked a question, avoid one-word answers. Most people will talk when others are friendly to them. Follow the leadership of the Holy Spirit as to when and how to transition into the subject of the gospel. Prepare transition statements in advance, such as, *"What is God doing in your life? "I learned something cool in Scripture today, can I tell you about it?" "Hey, let me tell you about a verse of Scripture that has really been speaking to me this week." "I was struggling a couple of years ago, let me tell you what changed that."* Or finally, you might say, *"Do you have a home church that you attend? If not, let me invite you to my church—maybe we could go out to lunch after the service this Sunday."*

COMMONLY ASKED DISCIPLESHIP QUESTIONS

How do I choose disciples?

The first step in establishing a formal disciple-making relationship is choosing disciples. Jesus, our example in selecting disciples, spent time in prayer before selecting men (Luke 6:12-16). The word *disciple* means *learner*. Begin by asking God to send you a group of men or women who have a desire to learn and grow.

When people approached Jesus about becoming His disciples, our Lord held a high standard. One man said, "I'll follow You, but let me go bury my father." Jesus said something like, "You can't do that. The kingdom is too important." Understand that the man's father had not yet died; he wanted to wait until after his father died.

Like Jesus's relationship with His disciples, ours is a serious relationship, a relationship built upon a mutual commitment to Christ and each other. Tragically, some will not follow through with that commitment, forcing you to confront them about their unfaithfulness. Occasionally, it may become necessary for you to ask someone to leave the group. In my years of leading D-Groups, on two occasions I've had to go to an unfaithful group member and say, "Listen, I love you, brother. I want to work with you, but at this stage in your life, your actions are telling me this is not a good time. Maybe we can meet in the future, when you are at a different place in your spiritual walk." As painful as this is, it rarely happens. But when it does, always be careful to handle it in a manner that edifies the uncommitted believer.

Your D-Group should consist of *F.A.T.* believers: Faithful, Available, and Teachable. A faithful person is dedicated, trustworthy, and committed. Consider a potential disciple's faithfulness by observing other areas of his/her spiritual life, such as church attendance, small group involvement, or service in the church. Faithfulness is determined by a commitment to spiritual things.

Discern an individual's availability by his willingness to meet with and invest in others. Does this person carve out time to listen, study, and learn from others? Is he accessible when called upon? Does she have a regular quiet time with God of reading the Word and praying? Availability is measured by a willingness to serve God.

Not everybody who attends a Bible study, Sunday school class, or D-Group is teachable. A teachable person has a desire to learn and apply what is taught. One who is teachable is open to correction. Recognize teachability by observing one's response to God's Word. For example, after hearing a sermon on prayer, does he begin to pray more regularly? Or after a lesson about the dangers of the tongue, does this person implement changes in her speech? A teachable person not only listens to what is taught, but also applies it to his or her life.

After discerning that an individual is faithful, available, and teachable, prayerfully approach him or her and ask, "Would you be interested in studying the

Bible together? Would you be interested in memorizing Scripture and praying together?" I have personally found that many people are open to that. All you have to do is ask. Never say, "Would you like for me to disciple you?" as this question may come across in a derogatory manner. Keep in mind, men should disciple men, and women should disciple women.

How many people should be in the group?

Because accountability works well in a smaller setting, the ideal size of a disciple-making group is three to five—you and two to four other people. Never have more than five, and remember that a one-on-one relationship is not ideal (see Chapter 3).

Where should we meet?

Find a meeting place away from the church. Restaurants, coffee shops, bookstores, diners, and homes are all good options. Meeting outside the church in the community forces your group to publicize your faith, teaching them it is okay to read the Bible at a restaurant or pray in public. Be sure to select a place that is convenient to all group members. I know stay-at-home moms who meet in each other's houses.

How often should we meet?

Ideally, you should meet once a week. You can meet more frequently, but it is important that you meet at least once a week. This schedule does not prohibit those you are discipling from calling you throughout the week or coming by for counsel when needed. Discipleship is an all-the-time, 24/7 commitment.

Is there an attendance requirement?

Yes, and it is not negotiable. The first time I meet with a potential group, I explain the disciple-making covenant with them. Since we're going to spend our lives together for the next twelve to eighteen months, I want to know if they are committed. Some people have said after the initial meeting, "Uh, this isn't really for me. I'm not interested." That's okay. I allow potential disciples to opt out of the group on the front end after understanding the expectations spelled out in the disciple-making covenant. Remember, you are looking for people who *want* to be discipled, people who have a desire to grow and learn. An unwillingness to commit reveals that they are not ready to be a disciple. It's the example Jesus set for us.

What do our meetings look like?

Begin with prayer. Ask each participant to present one prayer request at the start of each meeting. Assign a person to pray over the requests, and ask the Lord to sharpen each of you through your relationship.

Your weekly meetings should focus on four elements:

1. Study the Word together. Earlier in this book I outlined the H.E.A.R. method of studying the Bible: Highlight, Explain, Apply, Respond. Following this method will drive the group discussion.

2. Hold each person accountable for Scripture memory by reciting the previous week's passage before the group.

3. Ask accountability questions of each other. Hold each person accountable for achieving their goals. For example, "How is your relationship with Linda? You mentioned last week that you were working on the way you spoke to your wife."

4. Pray together before departing.

How do I dig deeper into the Bible?

In order to study the Bible in depth, you will use some study tools, beginning with a Bible dictionary. Early in our disciple-making relationship, David Platt gave me a Bible dictionary for my birthday. He said, "Robby, here's a gift that you'll use." And he was right. In addition to a Bible dictionary, it is important to have a good study Bible (the *ESV Study Bible*, the *MacArthur Study Bible*, and the *NIV Study Bible* include helpful commentary on each verse). If you can't afford to buy one of your own, you can access one on the Internet. Go to websites like BibleGateway.com, Bible.org, or BibleStudyTools.org. These are great resources. Additionally, Bible study software with a collection of helpful tools is very affordable.

How do I challenge my D-Group to memorize Scripture?

Proverbs 25:11 says, "*A word fitly spoken is like apples of gold in a setting of silver.*" How many times has a Scripture come to mind when you needed just the right words in a situation? Jesus promised that the Holy Spirit would bring to remembrance all that He said (John 14:26). Those passages of Scripture we have memorized will be brought to our memory at the right moment—but we must learn them.

Group members will memorize Scripture if you hold them accountable through reciting verses to one another at every meeting. See Chapter 8 for a thorough explanation and a practical system for Scripture memorization.

Should I disciple unbelievers?

I have led D-Groups with both believers and unbelievers present. My preferred method is a gathering of born-again believers seeking to grow in their faith. How do you determine if someone is saved or not? I begin every group by asking each person to share their testimony with the others. Next, ask them to explain the gospel. A great resource for anyone struggling with belief in Christ is Greg Gilbert's book, *What is the Gospel?* A few years ago, a guy in my group surrendered his life to Christ after six weeks of meeting because he "never understood the gospel prior to our meeting."

When should I ask someone to leave the D-Group?

I have asked only two people to leave our D-Group in nine years. Someone should be asked to leave the group for reasons such as these: they don't possess a teachable spirit, or they are not faithful in attending or completing the assigned work.

Teachability is an indispensable quality for growth. In one situation, I asked an individual to leave the group because he monopolized the discussion week after week. It was obvious he wanted to demonstrate his knowledge of the Word, rather than learn from interacting with others.

Additionally, laziness will breed complacency in the group. Missing meetings, refusing to memorize Scripture, failing to log H.E.A.R. entries, or sitting idly by during discussion times lowers the morale of the others in the group. This type of behavior must be addressed immediately. Meet with this individual privately to inquire about his/her attitude and actions. Remind him or her of the commitment made at the outset of the discipleship relationship.

Other reasons may require dismissing a group member. For example, a group member who is not trustworthy to maintain confidentiality or is judgmental toward others in the group may have to be removed.

What if I don't know the answer to a question?

I am often asked questions to which I don't know the answers. There is no shame in not knowing all the answers to every question. Simply confess that you may not have all the answers, but you will find them. Then do so before the next meeting. Ask your pastor or another spiritual leader to help you with the answer. Never give the impression that you have all the answers.

At the height of Henry Ford's popularity, people claimed that he was the smartest man in the world. During this time, a Chicago newspaper published a statement calling him an "ignorant pacifist." Ford fought the claim by suing the paper, which resulted in a trial landing him on the stand. Attorneys asked Ford questions on every subject imaginable, none of which he could answer. Exhausted from the questions, Ford ended the examination by stating, "If I should really want to answer the foolish question you have just asked, or any of the other questions you have been asking me, let me remind you that I have a row of electric push-buttons on my desk, and by pushing the right button, I can summon to my aid men who can answer any question I desire to ask concerning the business to which I am devoting most of my efforts. Now, will you kindly tell me, why I should clutter up my mind with general knowledge, for the purpose of being able to answer questions, when I have men around me who can supply any knowledge I require?"[88]

What he said was, "I am not the smartest man in the world because I know all the answers, but because *I know where to find the answers.*" You may not have total recall when it comes to biblical history, theology, and doctrine, but with time you can locate the answer.

When do I send out disciples to make disciples?

Always begin with the end in mind. Your group should meet for twelve to eighteen months. Some groups develop a closer bond, which results in accelerated growth; others take longer. The maximum time for meeting is two years. Some group members will desire to leave the group and begin their own groups. Others, however, will want to remain in the comfort zone of the existing group. Some will not want to start another group because of the sweet fellowship and bonds formed within the current group. Remember, the goal is for the men and women of the group to replicate their lives into someone else.

Paul, at the end of his life, commanded Timothy, *"And what you have heard from me in the presence of many witnesses, entrust to faithful men who are able to teach others also"* (2 Tim. 2:2). Within that one verse are four generations of disciple-making. Paul to Timothy is the first to second generation. Timothy to his disciples is the second to third generation. Timothy's disciples to others is the third to fourth generation. The goal of your group is to make disciples who will make disciples.

Jesus entrusted the greatest message in the world to twelve men, and one of them turned on Him. As a result of the commitment and faithfulness of the remaining eleven men, you are reading this book today. Disciple-making was Plan A. Jesus handed the baton to the disciples when he said, *"Go therefore and make disciples of all nations"* (Matt. 28:19). The apostles handed it to the early church fathers, who handed it down through the centuries. And now, the baton has been handed to you. Run with endurance. Eternity is at stake.

Appendix 10

SUGGESTED RESOURCES FOR D-GROUPS

Discipleship Resources

Adsit, Christopher B. *Personal Disciple-making: A Step-by-Step Guide for Leading a Christian From New Birth to Maturity.* Orlando, FL: Campus Crusade for Christ, 1996.

Arn, William and Charles Arn. *The Master's Plan for Making Disciples: Every Christian an Effective Witness through an Enabling Church.* 2nd ed. Grand Rapids, MI: Baker Books, 1982; 1998.

Arnold, Jeff. *The Big Book of Small Groups.* Downers Grove, IL: InterVarsity Press, 2004.

Barna, George. *Growing True Disciples.* Colorado Springs: WaterBrook Press, 2001.

Chan, Francis. *Multiply: Disciples Making Disciples.* Colorado Springs: David C. Cook, 2012.

Donahue, Bill. *Leading Life-Changing Small Groups.* Grand Rapids: Zondervan, 2002.

Donahue, Bill and Greg Bowman. *Coaching Life-Changing Small Group Leaders.* Grand Rapids: Zondervan, 2006.

Donahue, Bill and Russ Robinson. *Building a Church of Small Groups.* Grand Rapids: Zondervan, 2001.

_____. *The Seven Deadly Sins of Small Group Ministry.* Grand Rapids: Zondervan, 2002.

Eims, Leroy. *The Lost Art of Discipleship.* Grand Rapids: Zondervan, 1978.

Geiger, Eric, Michael Kelley, and Philip Nation. *Transformational Discipleship: How People Grow.* Nashville: Broadman and Holman Publishers, 2012.

Gorman, Julie A. *Community That is Christian.* Grand Rapids: Baker Book House, 2002.

Hull, Bill. *The Complete Book of Discipleship: On Being and Making Followers of Christ.* Colorado Springs, CO: NavPress, 2006.

_____. *The Disciple-Making Church: Leading a Body of Believers on a Journey of Faith, 2nd ed.* Grand Rapids: Baker Book House, 2010.

_____. *The Disciple-Making Pastor. Leading Others on a Journey of Faith, 2nd ed.* Grand Rapids: Baker Book House, 2007.

_____. *Jesus Christ: Disciplemaker, 2nd ed.* Grand Rapids: Baker Book House, 2004.

Icenogle, Gareth. *Biblical Foundations for Small Group Ministry.* Downers Grove, IL: InterVarsity Press, 1994.

Marshall, Collin and Tony Payne. *The Trellis and the Vine: The Ministry Mind-Shift that Changes Everything.* Kingsford, Australia: Matthias Media, 2009.

McCallum, Dennis and Jessica Lowery. *Organic Disciplemaking.* Houston, TX: Touch Outreach Ministries, 2006.

McBride, Neal. F. *How to Lead Small Groups.* Colorado Springs: NavPress, 1990.

Ogden, Greg. *Discipleship Essentials.* Downers Grove, IL: InterVarsity Press, 1998.

_____. *Transforming Discipleship: Making a Few Disciples at a Time.* Downers Grove, IL: InterVarsity Press, 2003.

Petersen, Jim. *Lifestyle Discipleship.* Colorado Springs: NavPress, 2007.

Platt, David. *Follow Me: A Call to Die. A Call to Live.* Carol Stream, IL: Tyndale House Publishers, Inc., 2013.

Putman, Jim, Bobby Harrington, and Robert Coleman, *DiscipleShift: Five Steps That Help Your Church to Make Disciples Who Make Disciples.* Grand Rapids: Zondervan, 2013.

Putman, Jim. *Real Life Discipleship*. Grand Rapids: Zondervan, 2010.

Rosenberg, Joel C. and Dr. T.E. Koshy. *The Invested Life: Making Disciples of all Nations One Person at a Time*. Wheaton, IL: Tyndale House Publishers, 2012.

Willard, Dallas. *The Great Omission*. San Francisco, CA: HarperCollins Publications, 2006.

Spiritual Disciplines Resources

Foster, Richard. *Celebration of Discipline: The Path to Spiritual Growth*. New York: HarperCollins, 1998.
Pettit, Paul, ed. *Foundations of Spiritual Formation*. Grand Rapids: Kregel, 2008.

Whitney, Donald. *Spiritual Disciplines for the Christian Life*. Colorado Springs: NavPress, 1991.

Wilhoit, James. *Spiritual Formation as if the Church Mattered*. Grand Rapids: Baker Academic, 2008.

Wilhoit, James and Kenneth O. Gangel, eds. *The Christian Educator's Handbook on Spiritual Formation*. Grand Rapids, MI: Baker Book House, 1994.

Willard, Dallas. *The Divine Conspiracy: Rediscovering our Hidden Life in God*. San Francisco: HarperCollins, 1997.

_____. *The Spirit of the Disciplines: Understanding How God Changes Lives*. San Francisco: HarperCollins, 1988.

Theology Resources

Grudem, Wayne and Jeff Purswell, ed. *Bible Doctrine.* Grand Rapids: Zondervan, 1999.

Grudem, Wayne and Eliot Grudem. *Christian Beliefs: Twenty Basic Beliefs Every Christian Should Know.* Grand Rapids, Zondervan, 2005.

Prayer Resources

Blackaby Henry and Norman Blackaby. *Experiencing Prayer with Jesus.* Eugene, OR: Multnomah Books, 2006.

Bounds, E. M. *The Classic Collection on Prayer.* Gainesville, FL: Bridge-Logos Publishers, 2001.

Foster, Richard J. *Prayer: Finding the Heart's True Home.* Downers Grove, IL: InterVarsity Press, 1992.

Murray, Andrew. *With Christ in the School of Prayer.* Peabody, MA: Hendrickson Publishers, 2007.

Whitney, Donald. *Spiritual Disciplines for the Christian Life.* Colorado Springs, CO: NavPress, 1994.

Bible Study Resources

Arthur, Kay. *How to Study the Bible: The Lasting Rewards of the Inductive Approach.* Eugene, OR: Harvest House Publishers, 1992.

Brand, Chad, Charles Draper, and Archie England. *Holman Illustrated Bible Dictionary.* Nashville, TN: Holman Bible Publishers, 1998.

Duvall, J. Scott, and J. Daniel Hays. *Grasping God's Word: A Hands-on Approach to Reading, Interpreting, and Applying the Bible,* 2nd ed. Grand Rapids: Zondervan, 2005.

Fee, Gordon D. and Douglas Stuart. *How to Read the Bible for All Its Worth, 3rd ed.* Grand Rapids: Zondervan, 1993.

_____. *How to Read the Bible Book by Book: A Guided Tour.* Grand Rapids, MI: Zondervan, 2002.

Hendricks, Howard G., and William D. Hendricks. *Living by the Book.* Chicago: Moody Press, 1991.

Klein, William W., Craig Blomberg, and Robert L. Hubbard. *Introduction to Biblical Interpretation.* Dallas: Word, 1993.

Kuhatschek, Jack. *Taking the Guesswork Out of Applying the Bible.* Downers Grove: InterVarsity Press, 1990.

Stein, Robert, H. *A Basic Guide to interpreting the Bible: Playing by the Rules.* Grand Rapids, MI: Baker, 1994.

Mickelsen, A. Merkeley. *Interpreting the Bible.* Grand Rapids, MI: Eerdmans Publishing, 1972.

Mounce, William D. *Mounce's Complete Expository Dictionary of Old and New Testament Words.* Grand Rapids: Zondervan, 2006.

Strong, James. *The New Strong's Exhaustive Concordance.* Nashville, TN: Thomas Nelson, 1990.

Zodhiates, Spiros. *The Complete Word Study Dictionary: Old Testament.* Chattanooga, TN: AMG Publishers, 1993.

_____. *The Complete Word Study Dictionary: New Testament.* Chattanooga, TN: AMG Publishers, 1992.

Websites

www.blueletterbible.org

www.bible.org

www.navpress/landing/discipleship/aspx

www.preceptaustin.org

Appendix 11

HOW TO PRAY FOR LOST FRIENDS

1. That they seek to know God. God has good plans for their lives – *"plans for welfare and not for calamity, to give them a future and a hope"* (Jer. 29:11). He promises to reveal Himself and His plans to those who seek Him wholeheartedly.

> *That they should seek God, in the hope that they might feel their way toward him and find him. Yet he is actually not far from each one of us."* (Acts 17:27)

> *But from there you will seek the LORD your God and you will find him, if you search after him with all your heart and with all your soul.* (Deut. 4:29)

2. That they believe the Scriptures. A non-Christian does not naturally understand the gospel. You must pray that the Holy Spirit will give them the understanding to believe the truth of His Word.

> *For the word of the cross is folly to those who are perishing, but to us who are being saved it is the power of God.* (1 Cor. 1:18)

3. That God will draw them to Himself. We must always remember that, although God uses us as the instruments to share the message and help lead people to Him, only God can convict and convert them. One cannot receive Christ until God first draws him. Let us therefore pray that God will draw our friends to Him.

"No one can come to me unless the Father who sent me draws him. And I will raise him up on the last day." (John 6:44)

4. That the Holy Spirit will work in them to turn from their sin and follow Christ as Lord. Be willing to let God work in their lives (Luke 15:17–18). Be bold enough to pray that God will cause things to come into their lives that will cause them to seek Him (Prov. 20:30).

And when he comes, he will convict the world concerning sin and righteousness and judgment. . . . When the Spirit of truth comes, he will guide you into all the truth, for he will not speak on his own authority, but whatever he hears he will speak, and he will declare to you the things that are to come. (John 16:8, 13)

Repent therefore, and turn again, that your sins may be blotted out. (Acts 3:19)

5. That God will send someone to lead them to Christ. Perhaps that someone is you. Pray that God will give you boldness to speak to them about Christ. Before you pray this prayer, be sure you mean it and will obey the Lord (Rom. 10:14–15).

Then he said to his disciples, "The harvest is plentiful, but the laborers are few; therefore pray earnestly to the Lord of the harvest to send out laborers into his harvest. (Matt. 9:37–38)

6. That they believe in and confess Christ as Savior and Lord. It is important that people understand that, in receiving Christ as Savior, they are also making Him the Lord of their lives. Pray that they will understand the seriousness of the commitment to receive Christ. Pray that they will come to grasp the scope of God's love. As their loving Father, He will never ask them to give up anything without giving them something far better in return.

But to all who did receive him, who believed in his name, he gave the right to become children of God. (John 1:12)

Because, if you confess with your mouth that Jesus is Lord and believe in your heart that God raised him from the dead, you will be saved. For with the heart one believes and is justified, and with the mouth one confesses and is saved. (Rom. 10:9–10)

BIBLIOGRAPHY

Absalom, Alex and Greg Nettle. *Disciples Who Make Disciples*. Exponential Resources, 2012 [e-book].

Adam, Peter. *Speaking God's Words: A Practical Theology of Preaching*. Leicester: InterVarsity Press, 1996.

Arthur, Kay. *How to Study Your Bible: The Lasting Rewards of the Inductive Approach*. Eugene, OR: Harvest House Publishers, 1992.

Barclay, William. *New Testament Words*. Louisville, KY: Westminster John Knox Press, 1974.

Bonhoeffer, Dietrich. *The Cost of Discipleship*. New York: Touchstone, 1937; 1995.

Breen, Mike and Steve Cockram. *Building a Discipling Culture*. Grand Rapids, MI: Zondervan Publishing House, 2009.

_____. *The Great Disappearance: Why the Word "Disciple" Disappears After Acts 21 and Why It Matters For Us Today*. Exponential Resources, 2013 [e-book].

Bridges, Jerry. *Holiness: Day by Day*. Colorado Springs, CO; Navpress; 2008.

Bright, Bill. *Witnessing Without Fear: How to Share Your Faith With Confidence*. Here's Life Publishers, Inc., 1987.

Browning, Dave. *Deliberate Simplicity*. Grand Rapids, MI: Zondervan, 2009.

Carraway, Bray. "Another Article on Finding the Will of God" Christianmagazine.org [Internet] http://sites.silaspartners.com/cc/article/0,,PTID42281_CHID787734_CIID216259000.html. Accessed 19 October 2012.

Christenson, Larry. *The Christian Family*. Minneapolis: Bethany House, 1970.

Christianity Today, "Willow Creek Repent?" http://blog.christianitytoday.com/outofur/archives/2007/10/willow_creek_re.html [online] (October 2007), Accessed 29 March 2013.

Coleman, Robert E. *Master Plan of Evangelism*. Grand Rapids, MI: Baker, 1963.

Cousins, Don and Judson Poling. *Discovering the Church: Becoming Part of God's New Community*. Grand Rapids, MI: Zondervan, 1992.

Dever, Mark. *The Gospel and Personal Evangelism*. Wheaton, IL: Crossway Books, 2007.

Dodson, Jonathan K. *Gospel Centered Discipleship*. Wheaton, IL: Crossway, 2012.

Duvall, J. Scott and J. Daniel Hays. *Grasping God's Word: A Hands-On Approach to Reading, Interpreting, and Applying the Bible*. Grand Rapids, MI: Zondervan, 2005.

_____. *Journey into God's Word: Your Guide to Understanding and Applying the Bible*. Grand Rapids, MI: Zondervan, 2008.

Edwards, David L. and John Stott. *Evangelical Essentials: A Liberal-Evangelical Dialogue*. London: Hodder & Stoughton Religious, 1988.

Foer, Joshua. *Moonwalking with Einstein: The Art and Science of Remembering Everything*. London: Penguin Books, 2011.

Forgetting Curve, http://www.festo-didactic.co.uk/gb-en/news/forgetting-curve-its-up-to-you.htm?fbid=Z2IuZW4uNTUwLjE3LjE2LjM0Mzc. [Internet] Accessed 21 March 2013.

Fukuda, Mitsuo. *Upward, Outward, Inward: Passing on the Baton of Discipleship*. Gloucester, UK: Wide Margin Books, 2010.

Gladwell, Malcolm. *Tipping Point*. Boston: MA: Little Brown & Co., 2002.

Graham, Billy. *The Holy Spirit*. Waco, TX: Word, 1978.

Grudem, Wayne A. *Systematic Theology: An Introduction to Biblical Doctrine*. Leicester, England; Grand Rapids, MI: Inter-Varsity Press, 2004.

Hendricks, Howard and William Hendricks. *As Iron Sharpens Iron*. Chicago: Moody Press, 1995.

Hill, Napoleon. *Think and Grow Rich*. Minneapolis, MN: Filiquarian Publishing, 1937.

Horbiak, Joan. *50 Ways to Lose Ten Pounds*. Lincolnwood, IL: Publications International, 1995.

Hull, Bill. *Disciplemaking Pastor: Leading Others on the Journey of Faith*. Ada: MI: Baker Books, 2007.

Jeremiah, David. "Testimonial Evidence" One Place http://www.oneplace.com/ministries/turning-point/read/articles/testimonial-evidence-13880.html. [Internet] Accessed 29 October 2012.

Kennedy, D. James. *Evangelism Explosion*, http://evangelismexplosion.org. [Internet] Accessed 15 May 2013.

Kimbro, Dennis. *What Makes the Great Great*. New York, NY: Random House, 2011.

Klein, William W., Craig L. Blomberg, and Robert I. Hubbard Jr. *Introduction to Biblical Interpretation*. Nashville, TN: Thomas Nelson, 2004.

Lewis, C. S. *Mere Christianity*. San Francisco, CA: Harper San Francisco, 2009.

Luter, Jr., Boyd. "Discipleship and the Church," *Bibliotheca Sacra Volume 137* (1980).

Malphurs, Aubrey. *Strategic Disciple Making: A Practical Tool for Successful Ministry*. Grand Rapids, MI: Baker Books, 2009.

Mandryk, Jason. *Operation World: The Definitive Prayer Guide to Every Nation*. Downers Grove, IL: IVP Books, 2012.

Murrell, Steve. *WikiChurch: Making Discipleship Engaging, Empowering, and Viral*. Lake Mary, FL: Charisma House Book Group, 2011.

"Nupedia," http://en.wikipedia.org/wiki/Nupedia. Accessed September 20, 2012.

Ogden, Greg. *Discipleship Essentials: A Guide to Building Your Life in Christ*. Downers Grove: IL: InterVarsity Press Books, 2007.

Olson, David T. "29 Interesting Facts about the America Church" http://www.theamericanchurch.org [online] (2006), Accessed 25 March 2013.

Ortberg, John. *The Life You've Always Wanted: Spiritual Disciplines for Ordinary People*. Grand Rapids, MI: Zondervan, 1997, 2002, Kindle Electronic Edition.

Osborne, Larry. *Sticky Church*. Grand Rapids, MI: Zondervan, 2008.

Peterson, Eugene. *Traveling Light*. Downers Grove, IL: InterVarsity Press 1982.

Phillips, J.B. *Phillips New Testament in Modern English*. New York, NY: Touchstone Books, 1958; 1996.

Pryor, Dwight. "Walk After Me" The Center for Judaic Christian Studies. [Internet] http://www.jcstudies.com. Accessed 15 October 2012.

Rainer, Thom S. and Jess S. Rainer, *The Millennials*. Nashville, TN: B & H Books, 2010.

Rosenberg, Joel C. and T. E. Koshy. *The Invested Life*. Carol Stream, IL: Tyndale House Publishers, 2012.

Spurgeon, Charles H. *Spurgeon's Sermons: Volume 28*, [Electronic ed.] Albany, OR: Ages Software, 1998.

Stratton, George M. "The Mnemonic Feat of the 'Shass Pollak,'" Psychological Review vol. 24 (May 1917).

Tozer, A. W. *Man, The Dwelling Place of God*. Milton Keynes, UK: Lightning Source Inc., 2008.

Veerman, Dave. *How to Apply the Bible*. Wheaton: Tyndale, 1993.

Watson, David. *Called and Committed*. Wheaton, IL: Harold Shaw, 1982.

What the Bible Says to the Believer. Chattanooga, TN: LMW Resources, 2012.

Whitney, Donald. *Spiritual Disciplines for the Christian Life*. Colorado Springs, CO: NavPress, 1991.

Wiersbe, Warren W. *5 Secrets of Living*. Wheaton, IL: Tyndale House, 1977.

Willard, Dallas. *The Great Omission*. San Francisco, CA: HarperCollins Publications, 2006.

Wuest, Kenneth S. *Wuest's Word Studies from the Greek New Testament*, Vol.2. Grand Rapids: Eerdmans, 1947.

ACKNOWLEDGMENTS

I am grateful to God for the measure of grace that He has given to complete this book. Many individuals worked countless hours to make this book a reality. I am indebted to Tim Lafleur, Doug Heller, and Jody Blaylock for encouraging me to write this book. Without the investment of Tim Lafleur and David Platt, I would not understand the concept of discipleship.

Tim and Gus Hernandez, Jr. met weekly with me for months outlining, organizing, and critiquing the material. Gus also provided the framework for the hermeneutics chapter.

I am grateful for the partnership with Randall Collins. Your tireless work shaping, molding, and developing ideas has made this book into what it is today. Also, I am grateful for the many people who contributed editorial insights: Len Allen, Whitney Coffman, Hal Stewart, Linda Brown, and Sam Rainer. I am grateful for the men in my discipleship groups over the past few years: Casey, Jesse, Jason, Jody, Nathan, Corey, Bryan, Trey, Ryan, Billy, Jared, Scott, Jonathan, John, Wiley, Sean, Michael, David, Clay, Rupe, Wesley, Dallas, Johnny, Corey, Jeff, and Paul. You were a sounding board during the creation and implementation phases of this book.

I am grateful for the board members of Replicate Ministries. Many of you supported me when others didn't. Your constant encouragement and support have spurred me on to complete this book. Also, I am thankful for the support and sacrifice Lori Meador made in the formative years of the ministry.

I am thankful for my family. Kandi, Rig, and Ryder have sacrificed to make this book a reality. Kandi, thank you for modeling discipleship in the church and in our home. Whether through sharing or showing the gospel to our boys or selflessly investing your life in a group of women weekly, you have displayed Christ's love. Also, I am grateful for my parents Bob and Margaret and my sister Lori who offered me a second chance 11 years ago. I am confident my life would be different today if you had not.

I am eternally thankful for the great salvation I have in Christ, for without Him, none of this would be possible. His grace sustains me daily. Paul's words to the church at Ephesus are more real today than ever before: *"Now to Him who is able to do far more abundantly than all that we ask or think, according to the power at work within us, to Him be glory in the church and in Christ Jesus throughout all generations, forever and ever. Amen"* (Eph. 3:20–21).

NOTES

1. "Forgetting Curve" http://www.festo-didactic.co.uk/gb-en/news/forgetting-curve-its-up-to-you.htm?fbid=Z2IuZW4u NTUwLjE3LjE2LjMwMzc. (Accessed 21 March 2013).

2. C. S. Lewis, *Mere Christianity* (San Francisco, CA: Harper San Francisco, 2009), 71–2.

3. Richard Mobbs, "Confucius and Podcasting" The University of Leicester, http://www.le.ac.uk/ebulletin-archive/ebulletin/features/2000-2009/2006/05/nparticle.2006-05-19.html. (Accessed 20 July 2013).

4. David T. Olson, "29 Interesting Facts about the America Church"http://www.theamericanchurch.org, 2006 (Accessed 25 March 2013).

5. Aubrey Malphurs, *Strategic Disciple Making: A Practical Tool for Successful Ministry* (Grand Rapids, MI: Baker Books, 2009), 25.

6. Christianity Today, "Willow Creek Repent?" http://blog.christianitytoday.com/outofur/archives/2007/10/willow_creek_re.html, October 2007, (Accessed 29 March 2013).

7. Ibid.

8. Jason Mandryk, *Operation World: The Definitive Prayer 8 to Every Nation* (Downers Grove, IL: IVP Books, 2012), 17.

9. Alex Absalom and Greg Nettle, *Disciples Who Make Disciples* (Exponential Resources, 2012), Kindle Electronic Edition: Location 104.

10. Chart was adapted from Greg Ogden, *Discipleship Essentials: A Guide to Building Your Life in Christ* (Downers Grove: IL: InterVarsity Press Books, 2007), 12.

11. Mitsuo Fukuda, *Upward, Outward, Inward: Passing on the Baton of Discipleship* (Gloucester, UK: Wide Margin Books, 2010), 100.

12. Jonathan K. Dodson, *Gospel Centered Discipleship* (Wheaton, IL: Crossway, 2012), Kindle Electronic Edition: Location 394–480.

13. Bill Hull, *Disciplemaking Pastor: Leading Others on the Journey of Faith* (Ada: MI: Baker Books, 2007), 54.

14. Ibid.

15. Boyd Luter Jr. "Discipleship and the Church," *Bibliotheca Sacra Volume 137* (1980), 272.

16. Mike Breen and Steve Cockram, *Building a Discipling Culture* (Grand Rapids, MI: Zondervan Publishing House, 2009), Kindle Electronic Edition: Location 100-101.

17. Eugene Peterson suggested that Jesus spent nine-tenths of his time on earth with the twelve disciples (See Eugene Peterson, *Traveling Light* (Downers Grove, IL: InterVarsity Press 1982), 182.

18. Hull, 169.

19. Mike Breen, *The Great Disappearance: Why the Word "Disciple" Disappears After Acts 21 and Why It Matters For Us Today* (Exponential Resources, 2013), Kindle Electronic Edition: Location 261–64.

20. Billy Graham, *The Holy Spirit* (Waco, TX: Word, 1978), 147.

21. Avery Willis, email received Monday, March 16, 2009, 4:14 p.m. He went on to say, "Now I am not against preaching. I do it all the time. My minor for my ThD was preaching. But Jesus chose twelve and lived with them, explained to them, gave them assignments, debriefed them, etc. to shape and mold them to be like Him. His sermons no doubt helped convey the truth, but he had to follow up most of it with what I call discipling."

22. Peter Adam, *Speaking God's Words: A Practical Theology of Preaching* (Leicester: InterVarsity Press, 1996), 59.

23. Steve Murrell, *WikiChurch: Making Discipleship Engaging, Empowering, and Viral* (Lake Mary, FL: Charisma House Book Group, 2011), 132–36.

24. Larry Osborne, *Sticky Church* (Grand Rapids, MI: Zondervan, 2008), 49.

25. Murrell, 134–35.

26. Dietrich Bonheoffer, *The Cost of Discipleship* (New York: Touchstone, 1937; 1995), 59.

27. Howard Hendricks and William Hendricks, *As Iron Sharpens Iron* (Chicago: Moody Press, 1995), 78.

28. David Watson, *Called and Committed* (Wheaton, IL: Harold Shaw, 1982), 53.

29. "Nupedia," http://en.wikipedia.org/wiki/Nupedia (Accessed September 20, 2012). This is the premise of Steve Murrell's book.

30. Murrell, 5.

31. Afterward, Bill explains that another student cannot take their final examination for them (it would never pass the accreditation requirements). However, he uses this illustration to provoke critical thinking about the goal of disciple-making.

32. Joel C. Rosenberg and T. E. Koshy, *The Invested Life* (Carol Stream, IL: Tyndale House Publishers, 2012), 35.

33. Malcolm Gladwell, *Tipping Point* (Boston: MA: Little Brown & Co., 2002), 173.

34. Don Cousins and Judson Poling, *Discovering the Church: Becoming Part of God's New Community* (Grand Rapids, MI: Zondervan, 1992), 50.

35. Jonathan K. Dodson, *Gospel Centered Discipleship* (Wheaton, IL: Crossway, 2012), Kindle Electronic Edition: Location 868-869.

36. Some manuscripts use 70 instead of 72 (see HCSB and NASB).

37. Ogden, 10.

38. I am in no way belittling the life changing moments you may have experienced in a one-on-one discipling relationship. However, it has been my experience at our church that a group of three to five is more likely to reproduce than a group of two.

39. Many years ago, Greg Ogden developed a disciple-making curriculum, which later became *Discipleship Essentials*, for his Doctor of Ministry project. He implemented the material in three different contexts, one-on-one, a group of three, and a group of ten to determine the ideal discipleship group size. The triad model for disciple-making surfaced from the study. For a more detailed explanation

see Greg Ogden, *Discipleship Essentials*.) Ogden identifies limitations with a one-on-one model.

40. Rosenberg and Koshy, 87–88.

41. Jerry Bridges, *Holiness: Day by Day* (Colorado Springs, CO: Navpress; 2008), 8

42. William Barclay, *New Testament Words* (Louisville, KY: Westminster John Knox Press, 1974), 107.

43. Kenneth S. Wuest, *Wuest's Word Studies from the Greek New Testament*, vol. 2 (Grand Rapids: Eerdmans, 1947), 213.

44. Donald Whitney, *Spiritual Disciplines for the Christian Life* (Colorado Springs, CO: Navpress, 1997), 24.

45. Ibid. 17–18.

46. J. B. Phillips, *Phillips New Testament in Modern English* (New York, NY: Touchstone Books, 1958; 1996).

47. John Ortberg, *The Life You've Always Wanted: Spiritual Disciplines for Ordinary People* (Grand Rapids, MI: Zondervan, 1997, 2002), Kindle Electronic Edition: Location 766–67.

48. Andrew Murray, *With Christ in the School of Prayer* (Whitaker House, 1981).

49. The book of Joshua identifies seven stone memorials in the land of Israel: Gilgal (Josh. 4:20), Achan (Josh. 7:26), King of Ai (Josh. 8:28–29), Copy of the Law (Joshua 8:30-32), Gibeon (Josh. 10:27), Gilead (Josh. 22:34), and Renewal of Covenant (Josh. 24:26–27).

50. Larry Christenson, *The Christian Family* (Minneapolis: Bethany House, 1970), 21.

51. Charles H. Spurgeon, *Spurgeon's Sermons: Volume 28*, [Electronic ed.] (Albany, OR: Ages Software, 1998).

52. Kay Arthur, *How to Study Your Bible: The Lasting Rewards of the Inductive Approach* (Eugene, OR: Harvest House Publishers, 1992).

53. J. Scott Duvall and J. Daniel Hays, *Journey into God's Word: Your Guide to Understanding and Applying the Bible* (Grand Rapids, MI: Zondervan, 2008), 119.

54. J. Scott Duvall and J. Daniel Hays, *Grasping God's Word: A Hands-On Approach to Reading, Interpreting, and Applying the Bible* (Grand Rapids, MI: Zondervan, 2005), 19–27.

55. Dave Veerman, *How to Apply the Bible* (Wheaton: Tyndale, 1993), 14.

56. William W. Klein, Craig L. Blomberg, and Robert I. Hubbard Jr., *Introduction to Biblical Interpretation* (Nashville, TN: Thomas Nelson, 2004), 471.

57. Dallas Willard, *The Great Omission* (San Francisco, CA: HarperCollins Publications, 2006), xi.

58. Hull, *Disciplemaking Pastor*.

59. Dwight Pryor, "Walk After Me" The Center for Judaic Christian Studies, http://www.jcstudies.com. (Accessed 15 October 2012).

60. A. W. Tozer, *I Call It Heresy* (Wingspread, new edition, 2010).

61. Leroy Eims, *The Lost Art of Discipleship* (Grand Rapids: Zondervan, 1978).

62. Warren W. Wiersbe, *5 Secrets of Living* (Wheaton, IL: Tyndale House, 1977), 62–79.

63. Ibid., 79.

64. Dave Browning, *Deliberate Simplicity* (Grand Rapids, MI: Zondervan, 2009), Kindle Electronic Edition: Location 515–18.

65. Bray Carraway, "Another Article on Finding the Will of God" Christianmagazine.org; http://sites.silaspartners.com/cc/article/0,,PTID42281_CHID787734_CIID2162590,00.html. (Accessed 19 October 2012).

66. Donald Whitney, *Spiritual Disciplines for the Christian Life* (Colorado Springs, CO: NavPress, 1991), 21.

67. George M. Stratton "The Mnemonic Feat of the 'Shass Pollak,'" *Psychological Review* vol. 24, (May 1917) 244–47.

68. Joshua Foer, *Moonwalking with Einstein: The Art and Science of Remembering Everything* (London: Penguin Books, 2011), 109.

69. Whitney, 59.

70. Thomas Watson, *Puritan Sermons,* vol. 2 (Wheaton, IL: Richard Owen Roberts, 1674; 1981), 62.

71. Twitter, 9:27 am. (Accessed 19 January 2013), @derwinlgray.

72. Robert E. Coleman, *Master Plan of Evangelism* (Grand Rapids, MI: Baker, 1963), 21.

73. Bill Bright, *Witnessing Without Fear: How to Share Your Faith With Confidence* (Here's Life Publishers, Inc., 1987), 67.

74. Wayne A. Grudem, *Systematic Theology: An Introduction to Biblical Doctrine* (Leicester, England; Grand Rapids, MI: InterVarsity Press; Zondervan, 2004), 704.

75. See Thom S. Rainer and Jess S. Rainer, *The Millennials* (Nashville, TN: B&H Books, 2010).

76. Ed Stetzer "Preach the Gospel, and Since It's Necessary, Use Words" http://www.christianitytoday.com/edstetzer/2012/june/preach-gospel-and-since-its-necessary-use-words.html. (Accessed 2 July 2013).

77. Mark Dever, *The Gospel and Personal Evangelism* (Wheaton, IL: Crossway Books, 2007), 43.

78. A. W. Tozer, *Man, The Dwelling Place of God* (Milton Keynes, UK: Lightning Source Inc. 2008), 11.

79. Paul Gilbert, as quoted by David Jeremiah, "Testimonial Evidence" One Place, http://www.oneplace.com/ministries/turning-point/read/articles/testimonial-evidence-13880.html. (Accessed 29 October 2012).

80. David L. Edwards and John Stott, *Evangelical Essentials: A Liberal-Evangelical Dialogue* (London: Hodder & Stoughton Religious, 1988), 329.

81. Joan Horbiak, *50 Ways to Lose Ten Pounds* (Lincolnwood, IL: Publications International, 1995), 95. Although this saying circulated years before, it was attributed to Saint Exupéry around 2007.

82. I adapted the H.E.A.R. journal from the Life Journal. For more details see www.lifejournal.cc.

83. Robert L. Sumner, *The Wonder of the Word of God* (Biblical Evangelism Press, 1969).

84. Dennis Kimbro, *What Makes the Great Great* (New York, NY: Random House, 2011), 133.

85. *What the Bible Says to the Believer* (Chattanooga, TN: Leadership Ministries Worldwide, 2012).

86. Will Allen Dromgoole, "Bridge Builders" as cited in Greg Ogden *Discipleship Essentials: A Guide to Building Your Life in Christ* (Downers Grove: IL: InterVarsity Press Books, 1998).

87. D. James Kennedy, *Evangelism Explosion*, http://evangelismexplosion.org. (Accessed 15 May 2013).

88. Napoleon Hill, *Think and Grow Rich* (Minneapolis, MN: Filiquarian Publishing, 1937; 1985), 108.

ABOUT THE AUTHOR

Robby Gallaty is the senior pastor of Long Hollow Baptist Church in Hendersonville, Tennessee. He was radically saved out of a life of drug addiction on November 12, 2002. In 2008, he began Replicate Ministries to equip and train men and women to be disciples who make disciples. He is also the author of *Creating An Atmosphere to Hear God Speak* (2009), *Unashamed: Taking a Radical Stand for Christ* (2010), *Growing Up: How to Be a Disciple Who Makes Disciples* (2013), *Firmly Planted: How to Cultivate a Faith Rooted in Christ* (2015), *Rediscovering Discipleship: Making Jesus's Final Words Our First Work* (2015), *MARCS of a Disciple* (2016), *The Forgotten Jesus: Why Western Christians Should Follow an Eastern Rabbi* (2017), *Recovered* (2019), and *Replicate* (2020).

Develop a discipleship plan

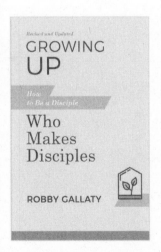

Revised and Updated

GROWING UP

How to Be a Disciple

Who
Makes
Disciples

ROBBY GALLATY

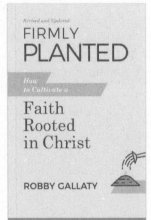

Revised and Updated

FIRMLY PLANTED

How to Cultivate a

Faith
Rooted
in Christ

ROBBY GALLATY

Revised and Updated

BEARING FRUIT

What Happens When

God's
People
Grow

ROBBY GALLATY

AVAILABLE WHERE BOOKS ARE SOLD.

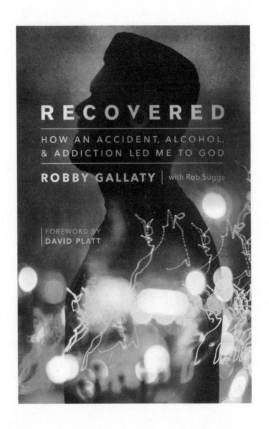